ORDER BOOK
OF THE
HESSE-CASSEL VON MIRBACH REGIMENT

Bruce E. Burgoyne
Edited by Dr. Marie E. Burgoyne

HERITAGE BOOKS
2008

HERITAGE BOOKS
AN IMPRINT OF HERITAGE BOOKS, INC.

Books, CDs, and more—Worldwide

For our listing of thousands of titles see our website at
www.HeritageBooks.com

Published 2008 by
HERITAGE BOOKS, INC.
Publishing Division
100 Railroad Ave. #104
Westminster, Maryland 21157

Copyright © 2004 Bruce E. Burgoyne and Dr. Mary E. Burgoyne

All rights reserved. No part of this book may be reproduced or transmitted in any form or by any means, electronic or mechanical, including photocopying, recording or by any information storage and retrieval system without written permission from the author, except for the inclusion of brief quotations in a review.

International Standard Book Numbers
Paperbound: 978-0-7884-2530-1
Clothbound: 978-0-7884-7057-8

OTHER HERITAGE BOOKS BY BRUCE E. BURGOYNE:

A Hessian Officer's Diary of the American Revolution Translated From An Anonymous Ansbach-Bayreuth Diary and The Prechtel Diary

Canada During the American Revolutionary War: Lieutenant Friedrich Julius von Papet's Journal of the Sea Voyage to North America and the Campaign Conducted There

CD: Ansbach-Bayreuth Diaries from the Revolutionary War

CD: The Hessian Collection, Vol. 1: Revolutionary War Era

Defeat, Disaster, and Dedication

Diaries of Two Ansbach Jaegers

Diary of a Hessian Grenadier of Colonel Rall's Regiment Written by Johannes Reuber

Eighteenth Century America: (A Hessian Report On the People, the Land, the War) As Noted in the Diary of Chaplain Philipp Waldeck (1776-1780)

Enemy Views: The American Revolutionary War as Recorded by the Hessian Participants

Georg Pausch's Journal and Reports of the Campaign in America, as Translated from the German Manuscript in the Lidgerwood Collection in the Morristown Historical Park Archives, Morristown, NJ

Hesse-Hanau Order Books, A Diary and Roster: A Collection of Items Concerning the Hesse-Hanau Contingent of "Hessians" Fighting Against the American Colonists in the Revolutionary War

Hessian Chaplains: Their Diaries and Duties

OTHER HERITAGE BOOKS BY BRUCE E. BURGOYNE
(continued):

Journal of the Hesse-Cassel Jaeger Corps

Mirbach Order Book: Order Book of the Hesse-Cassel von Mirbach Regiment

Most Illustrious Hereditary Prince: Letters to Their Prince from Members of Hesse-Hanau Military Contingent in the Service of England During the American Revolution

Notes from a British Museum

The Battle of Brandywine, 11 September 1777

The Battle of Guilford Courthouse and the Siege and Surrender at Yorktown by Berthold Koch

The Diary of Lieutenant von Bardeleben and Other von Donop Regiment

The Hesse-Cassel Mirbach Regiment in the American Revolution

The Third English-Waldeck Regiment in the American Revolutionary War

The Trenton Commanders: Johann Gottlieb Rall and George Washington, as noted in Hessian Diaries

Introduction

The Order Book of the Hesse-Cassel Mirbach Regiment is an ideal companion piece to *The Hesse-Cassel Mirbach Regiment in the American Revolution*, Heritage Books, Inc. (Bowie, MD, 1995). It is an excellent source of information on promotions and transfers throughout the Hessian army, and provides a picture of the daily life in an infantry regiment.

Several notes indicate portions of the German manuscript that I have not translated for a variety of reasons, none of which makes the translation of less value.

The Mirbach Regiment was part of the 1st Division of Hesse-Cassel troops which sailed for America in 1776, and it remained in America until the end of the war. The most significant role in combat was during the attack on Fort Mercer in New Jersey in October 1777, when the regiment took serious losses.

The Order Book ends in 1780 at which time the unit was redesignated the Jung von Lossberg Regiment.

As with all my translations, I recommend that the readers return to the German manuscript to verify my translation.

In previous translations I have given my wife credit for her assistance, but her assistance has reached the point where a sincere thank you is not enough. Therefore, I have acknowledged her contributions by crediting her as the editor of the finished product. Nevertheless, thank you, Marie.

Bruce E. Burgoyne
Dover DE, 2003

Mirbach Order Book

Order Book
Of the
Hesse-Cassel von Mirbach Regiment

<u>New York, 19 March 1777</u>

On the gracious orders of His Serene Highness, the illustrious Hessian troops under my command are herewith informed of the following occurrences and of His Highness' pleasure in making known the gracious changes and promotions.

- - - - - - - -

According to the gracious letter
Dated, Weissenstein, 27 October 1776

1) General of the Infantry and Governor [Heinrich Wilhelm] Wutginau has died, but his regiment will retain its rank and designated place among battalions, pending further determination.

2) Major General von Marschall, of the Prince Friedrich Regiment, has also died, and Colonel von Buttlar, a member of that unit, has been named commander in his place.

3) Major von Urff, of the Leib [Body[Dragoon Regiment, is promoted to lieutenant colonel; Major von Stahl is transferred from the Prince Friedrich Regiment in his place; and Captain von Todtenwarth, of the latter regiment, is also promoted to major, with the reservation that older captains retain seniority.

1

Mirbach Order Book

4) Captains von Wutginau and von Waitz, serving as 1st lieutenants in the 1st Guard Battalion, are promoted to major with the reservation that older captains retain seniority.

5) Major General Georg von Balcke has reentered the service and been given the 2nd Battalion of the von Huyn Regiment as his own special garrison regiment, with his name.

6) Major [Johann Adolf] von Eschtruth has also reentered service as a lieutenant colonel in the 2nd Battalion of the von Stein Regiment. Also, Captain [Johann Jacob] Koehler, of the Prince Friedrich Dragoon Regiment, is assigned as lieutenant colonel of the 2nd Battalion of the von Wissenbach Regiment. Captain Porbeck of the Balcke Garrison Regiment, is promoted to major in the same, with the reservation that older captains retain seniority; and Captain [Johann Eckhard] Bode, of the Schlotheim Dragoon Regiment, is promoted to major in the 2nd Battalion of the von Buenau Regiment.

- - - - - - - -

Also, according to the garrison letter
Dated, Cassel, 29 November 1776

1) The Vacant von Wutginau Regiment has been designated the Landgraf Regiment, and at all times has precedence after the Leib Infantry Regiment.

2) This, and at the same time, other changes to the previous ranking of the battalions require the present

Mirbach Order Book

situation to be observed until further communications are made.

3) Colonel [Heinrich Anton] von Herringen is named commander of the mentioned Landgraf Regiment and in his place

4) Colonel [Johann August] von Loos is named commander of the von Lossberg Regiment, and in his place

5) Colonel [Justus Heinrich] Block is named commander of the Mirbach Regiment.

6) Being replaced by Lieutenant Colonel (Georg Emanuel von] Lengercke, of the Prince Charles Regiment, who is transferred to the Grenadier Battalion.

7) Major DuPuy is transferred to the von Truembach Regiment.

8) Major General von Welcke is promoted to lieutenant general, and

9) Major General von Hackenberg is designated as deputy commandant at Rheinfels.

At the same time, notice is given that Colonel Block has been given the *Orden pour la virtu Militaire* and also that the conduct of the Hessian troops in the Battle of Long Island on 27 August [1776], and after the landing on York [Manhattan] Island on 15 September [1776] have earned His Serene Highness' fullest approbation.

When young gentlemen are recommended for

Mirbach Order Book

commissions, their ages must always be noted.

Von Heister

- - - - - - -

Order of Battle
Lieutenant General [Leopold] von Heister
Major General [Werner] von Mirbach

Mirbach, Donop, Prince Charles, Landgraf, (Regiments), and von Minnigerode Grenadier Battalion

Major General [Johann Daniel] Stirn

Von Linsing Grenadier Battalion, and Leib, Herditary Prince, Ditfurth, and Truembach (Regiments)

Lieutenant General [Wilhelm] von Knyphausen

Colonel [Friedrich Wilhelm] von Lossberg

Huyn, Stein, and von Knyphausen (Regiment), and Koehler Grenadier Battalion

Major General [Martin] Schmidt

Von Lengercke Grenadier Battalion, and Lossberg, Rall, Wissenbach, and Buenau (Regiments)

- - - - - - -

Extract from the gracious letter
Of His Highness
Dated Cassel, 7 April 1777

Accustomed as I am to value the honor of my troops in all situations, I could receive no more grievous and unhappy report, than that, in an unfortunate moment, I lost three regiments which had well-earned and long-maintained reputations.

Nothing but the complete neglect of order and discipline could have caused this disgrace. And I live in the firm hope, that as I also need to find a way to remove the pain of such a catastrophe, the same [a marginal note of unknown origin seems to indicate von Heister is meant] will not rest until my troops have removed the memory of this unfortunate incident by numerous praiseworthy accomplishments.

Colonel [Johann Gottlieb] Rall's death has saved him from his just desserts, but unbounded punishment is justified to those who, after his fatal wound, ordered the laying down of arms by the battalions they commanded and dishonored the Hessian name at this shameful place, instead of at least seeking to at least fight their way out like true soldiers, when the place could no longer be defended. Most of those who fled from these regiments show what the rest could have done, if the remaining officers had remembered their duty, and not put aside what they owed me, the honor of my corps and themselves.

The particulars of this disgrace are unknown to me at this time. However, no report has been received which would indicate otherwise. I hereby order the lieutenant general to closely question all the officers upon their return and to submit to me an exact report of the incident.

I see myself compelled to make an example of the

guilty individuals, and now declare that these regiments shall never again receive flags until they have recaptured from the enemy a number equal to those which they lost in such a shameful manner.

With constant esteem, the lieutenant general remains, in the full affection of
Friedrich, Landgrave of Hesse

- - - - - - -

According to the gracious letter
Of His Highness, 8 May 1777

Captain [Karl Wilhelm] von Eschwege of the Linsing Grenadier Battalion is promoted to major of the Guard Regiment, and his grenadier company is awarded to Captain Verna.

Commanders of regiments are given the strictest orders to submit the appropriate reports and rank listings containing detailed explanations, no longer every three month, as previously ordered, but because of the long and uncertain crossing, as often as the departure of a ship provides an opportunity.

The vacant Rall Regiment is awarded to Colonel [Wolfgang Friedrich] von Woellwarth as of 13 May.

Lieutenant Colonel [Karl] von Kitzel is not to be assigned to the Stein Regiment as previously resolved, but to the Wissenbach Regiment in which he gets the Horn Company.

The Schrievogel Company of the Stein Regiment goes to Captain [Friedrich] Platte of that Regiment.

Mirbach Order Book

Captain von Verna, having taken his discharge, does not receive the Eschwege Company of the Linsing Grenadier Battalion, but it goes to Captain [Karl August] von Plessen, who sails with the present shipment, with which Captain [Henrich Karl] von Webern departs, in order to take over the Grenadier Company of the mentioned battalion, which Major [Karl] von Wurmb, who has been transferred to the Donop Regiment, has had.

Colonel [Karl] von Bose is named commander of the Landgraf Regiment, and Lieutenant Colonel [Maximilian] von Westerhagen is promoted to Colonel of the Ditfurth Regiment in his place, having sailed with the latest shipment, also.

The necessary men will be taken from the regiments' five musket companies to serve as replacements for vacancies in the Grenadier Battalions.

The 16th of June - Lieutenant Colonel [Karl Philipp] Heymel is transferred to the Knyphausen Regiment and awarded the vacant Dechow Company.

Lieutenant General [Wilhelm Henrich August] von Donop and likewise Lieutenant General [Anton Friedrich] von Lossberg are not to be carried as sick, but as in command.

In the event that the Hessian troops are separated from Lieutenant General von Knyphausen, the commanding generals or brigadiers of the distant regiments and brigades will, in the future, immediately send their reports and lists with the first ship departing from their regions, to His Highness.

Lieutenant Colonel [Hans Henrich] Eitel is to send in his lists and reports about the Artillery Corps in America each month.

Despite their previous duties, as long as they are in the hospital, nothing can be done concerning deductions from the pay of non-commissioned officers who are in the hospital.

The following promotions and transfers are announced:

Promoted to major general are:
Colonel von Lossberg of the Leib Infantry Regiment
Colonel von Bose of the Landgraf
Colonel von Jungkenn of the 1st Guard Regiment
Colonel von Buttlar of the Prince Friedrich Regiment

Colonel [Johann Ludwig] von Horn is transferred from the 1st to the 2nd Wissenbach Battalion.

Colonel von Woellwarth is awarded the vacant Rall Grenadier Battalion and Colonel von Hanstein is retired on pension

Lieutenant Colonel von Westerhagen of the Guard Regiment is promoted to colonel of the Ditfurth Regiment.

Promoted to lieutenant colonel are:
  Major von Lengsfeld of the Wilcke Regiment
  Major [Karl] Kitzel of the Wissenbach Regiment
  Major Freudenberg of the Guard Regiment
  Major Schmidt of the Heister Regiment
  Major Schreiber of the Hussars
  Major Schenck of the Gens d'Arms [militia ?]

Lieutenant Colonel Heymel is transferred from the Donop to the Knyphausen Regiment; Lieutenant Colonel [August Ernst Wilhelm von] Schreivogel from the 1st to the 2nd Stein Battalion.

Promoted to major are:
  Captain [Melchior] Martini of the Huyne Regiment
  Captain Carl von Wurmb of the Guard Regiment, and transferred to the Donop Regiment
  Captain Ludwig von Schollen of the Wilcke Regiment
  Rittmeister [Captain] Helmerich of the Gens d'Arms.

In the future, chiefs and commanders of regiments shall recommend no free corporals or other young persons as officers who have not attained seventeen years of age. No one who is

Mirbach Order Book

not fifteen years old and possessed of the necessary qualifications shall be accepted in the regiment as a free corporal, and even less so, as a supernumerary, those who can be even less effectively utilized.

Colonels [Johann Christoph] von Huyn and [Johann Wilhelm] Schreiber, because of demonstrated performance on several occasions and their good reputations are awarded the "Orden pour la vertu Militaire."

Captain [Friedrich Ernst] von Muenchhausen of the Lossberg Regiment is transferred to and awarded the regimental grenadier company, and further more, is named an aide-de-camp to His Highness.

Captains [Johann August] von Westerhagen, Ernst von Eschwege, and [Johannes] von Groening of the Linsing Grenadier Battalion are to return to the Guard Regiment this year, and three other lieutenants will be assigned in their stead. However, as these can not be sent out with a future outbound shipment, the three mentioned captains are to remain with their troops, awaiting further orders.

In the event native born Americans are found who offer to volunteer their services as soldiers, these persons can be accepted into the regiment as privates if there is nothing else against their

Mirbach Order Book

enlistment, and when peace is restored, can return to Hesse with the regiments.

Mirbach Order Book

1778

The 1st of January - Regimental Orders

1) Companies must take care of items delivered to them, because if something should be lost, the company commander must replace it.

2) If someone, who has been left behind on assignment in the country dies, he is immediately to be so reported to the regimental quartermaster.

3) In the future, the staff guard mount will be held at eleven o'clock.

4) In the immediate future, the quarters are to be changed, the companies spread out more, and more houses assigned.

5) The regimental surgeon is to visit the companies, and sick individuals, twice weekly, Mondays and Thursdays, and report each time to the colonel and major.

6) As it has been found necessary to maintain a picket of a private 1st class and three men between the detachment at Blumenthal and Major Wilmowsky's Company, the picket is to be provided by Major von Wilmowsky's Company, which henceforth will not be required to provide men for the staff guard.

The 2nd of January - The invalid lists are to be given to General Schmidt.

The 3rd of January - At eight o'clock in the morning sufficient wagons will be assembled at that place where wood for the staff was received recently.

The 4th of January - As today's orders are to contain a list of the total losses of those killed, of those dead from disease, deserters, etc., sent in since departure from Hesse, the companies must send, as noted above, a list to the adjutant. Officers are to be noted by name. At eight o'clock in the morning, all the wagons, plus a captain-at-arms and four men are to report to the regimental quartermasters' quarters to pick up the uniforms in the city. Companies are to report those troops considered invalids. The regimental surgeon will attest thereto, and after a complete examination and approval, the generals and colonels will send it on to General Schmidt.

The 5th of January - It is strictly forbidden to chop down or burn fences or fruit trees, or break into houses for gain, and upon the least damage being reported, the colonel will hold the company commanders responsible. Therefore, the company commanders must give the strictest orders that their troops accept no wood but that which is issued, as this may be charged to the regiment, and in such cases the company commanders will have to pay for it.

At nine o'clock tomorrow the personal effects of Colonel [Ernst Rudolf] von Schieck and the other officers, who were killed, will be inventoried.

The 6th of January - Nothing.

The 7th of January - Complaints having been

Mirbach Order Book

received from the inhabitants, that the companies are taking their wood allowances before they are measured out. It is the colonel's order, that on the threat of the most severe punishment, such should not happen again, but that it be measured each time and issued according to directions.

The 8th of January - Nothing.

The 9th of January - Company commanders will insure that their sick in the hospital are provided with at least a good shirt, as Doctor Lauchhard has made a complaint to the colonel about this point. The new trousers may be issued to the troops, but the company commanders will pay strict attention to insure that the trousers are properly cared for, and not worn except when absolutely necessary.

The 10th of January - Nothing.

The 11th of January - All the new uniform items will be issued to the men who are present tomorrow, but the colonel orders, that with the threat of the most severe punishment, no non-commissioned officer or private presume to use a single item therefrom, as this issue is necessary only to prevent loss in case a fire should occur in the company commander's quarters. Officers are ordered to check the equipment each time the quarters are inspected, and the non-commissioned officers and corporals are responsible for the men keeping the equipment safe and clean. If an alert occurs and the regiment must move out, the items will be placed in front of the company commander's quarters by the men, where they will be loaded on wagons, and the captain-at-arms will be left with a command to guard them. The equipment for missing individuals and the sick will be the responsibility of the company commanders.

The 12th and 13th of January - Nothing.

The 14th - The companies will complete lists according to the accompanying format, and send them to me as soon as possible, as War Councilor Lorenz requires them at once. Notice should be taken

    1) That losses at Red Bank be shown under the column, and the names of soldiers who are missing must be expressly noted.

    2) Nothing is to be listed except that which was truly lost at Red Bank.

    3) All the company officers are to sign on their sworn honor and to affirm this with their seal.

The 15th, 16th, 17th, 18th, and 19th - Nothing.

The 20th of January - The regiment will provide one non-commissioned officer and six privates daily. They will assemble each morning at precisely ten o'clock before Lieutenant [Ludwig Wilhelm August] von Boyneburg's quarters, where they will report for duty.

The regiment is notified that if rockets are fired near the Morris house, it will be the alarm system. Lieutenant Colonel [Wilhelm] von Loewenstein will

Mirbach Order Book

give notice of such to the detachment at the nearest regimental post, all of which must be notified by calling out to the next post, so that the staff and all the companies present can receive the information at once.

<u>The 21st of January</u> - As Lieutenant Colonel [Friedrich von] Porbeck has informed me of the unpleasant report that non-commissioned officers, as well as privates, of the Wissenbach Regiment are carousing, drinking, and starting fights. It is therefore ordered that on fear of the strictest punishment, that if either non-commissioned officers or privates are found in such condition, they will be arrested and brought to the staff watch as prisoners for further punishment.

Furthermore, the adjutant has informed me that some 1st sergeants have not established a fixed time for submitting the required lists and reports, and even the payday and required Saturday reports are not received on time, which latter is especially the greatest neglect. Therefore, all 1st sergeants are notified that the first one about whom a complaint is received, will be placed in arrest at the staff watch, and will be locked in stocks for 24 hours.

von Borck

<u>The 22nd of January</u> - Nothing.

<u>The 23rd of January</u> - As pay is to be given out on the 26th, the colonel orders that all company commanders assemble their companies, and check that the troops have their weapons in good condition,

Mirbach Order Book

their leather colored, and everything in polished and proper condition, also that their cartridges are well-cared for and have not been damaged.

The 24th and 25th - Nothing.

The 26th of January - Despite the frequently repeated orders that no non-commissioned officer or soldier is to be on the streets of New York at night, this is still prevalent, and they run around drunk and committing excesses. Therefore the colonel again forbids such behavior on threat of punishment by running the gauntlet, and informs company commanders that he holds them accountable should the least excess occur, and the non-commissioned officers must be held more responsible for inspecting their troops, and thereby prevent the running around.

The 27th - Nothing.

The 28th - As the colonel has been informed that some companies have generally been supplied with black cloth leggings, he hopes that the troops have also been supplied with black linen leggings, so that when the regiment is assembled together, there is no variation therein, and that all companies are the same, and are wearing black leggings of the same sort.

As the colonel has received a most serious complaint from Mr. Kemble that in his house, where the staff watch is located, on two different occasions, some days ago, his private rooms were broken into, a cabinet opened, and stockings, jackets, pants, and money were stolen. In all probability, the guard itself committed the theft because the soldiers quartered there were closely inspected, and nothing was found. Therefore the colonel orders all company commanders to conduct a thorough investigation to see if it is possible to solve this terrible deed, the breaking in, not only to prevent farther complaints by Mr. Kemble, which seems likely to occur, but also to protect the regiment from the disadvantageous reputation that it has no discipline.

The 29th of January - Nothing.

The 30th of January - The company commanders will insure that their wagon horses are used for no other purpose except regimental duties, and that the forage for the horses is not diverted to other use.

The 31st of January - General Schmidt orders that during the present mild weather, the recruits and clumsy individuals be drilled extensively.

February

The 1st, 2nd, and 3rd - Nothing.

The 4th - It has been learned that some soldiers when relieved from guard duty, have shot ducks on their way back, so the colonel orders that every time the officers inspect the quarters, they will check the cartridges, and strictly forbid the soldiers using the same, and keep a close watch on them.

A complaint has again been received that during

Mirbach Order Book

the past night, all the garden fruit was stolen from a man near the colonel's quarters. The companies will investigate at once to see if they can determine who committed this act. At the same time, it is to be reported that the local inhabitants have been supplied with weapons, and may use them.

The 5th of February - General Schmidt orders the regimental company commanders to immediately make an effort to close the pay accounts for the soldiers for the past year, and as soon as this is done, the company chiefs will report it to General Schmidt.

The 6th - Nothing.

The 7th - The Hessian artillery officer is to go as a relief into Fort Independence, and remain there fourteen days.

Brigade Orders

To be submitted to War Councilor Lorenz:

1) The lost list, including officers, non-commissioned officers, medics, and privates from the departure from Hesse to the end of 1777.

2) The invalid list.

3) The regimental quartermasters will submit the provisions and forage rations [issued] since departure from Hesse, by months. Officers will be listed by name, the others summarized.

4) What soldier deposits [Consengelder] has been received.

5) Which promoted officers are attached to

Mirbach Order Book

Carlshafen Hospital.
    6) The financial accounts owing to dead officers, and where the monies are.
    The 8th - Nothing.
    The 9th - As disgusting excesses have been committed by the Hessian regiments lying in quarters here, as well as outside the city, especially at night, and because the bad behavior of the privates and soldiers toward the English can only lead to revenge, General Schmidt orders the regimental commanders to order their company commanders to keep a better watch over their troops, to frequently check the troops in their night quarters, and to allow no soldiers to be seen on the street after seven o'clock, in order to keep better watch on the houses where the soldiers are quartered, guards will be posted from the sentry force. Those houses shall be constantly patrolled, and all those soldiers arrested, who are caught in the street after the set time. This order will be made known to each man, with the understanding that the soldiers who disobey will be severely punished.

<u>Regimental Order</u>

As it has come to the colonel's attention that some officers not only leave their quarters without permission, but also remain in New York all night, and this against standing orders, this is to notify all officers that should this occur again, the officers will be placed in arrest, and General von Mirbach notified.

Mirbach Order Book

The colonel also orders that no non-commissioned officer or private is to be granted leave to go into the city in the future, except on Wednesdays and Saturdays, which are market days, when they can buy necessities. Except for those times, no one is to go to New York, and the company commanders will give the strictest orders that no privates or non-commissioned officers shall go there, and if they do, they will be sent in arrest, to the staff watch.

The 10th, 11th, 12th, and 13th - Nothing.

The 14th - As the forage money is to be paid to the officers here, through the end of 1777, or 165 days, an exact list is to be sent to War Councilor Lorenz by the regiments, including those officers on command, or already named, but who have not yet reported to the regiment. Artillery officers, and general staff personnel are to be noted also.

In accordance with an order received from His Excellency, Lieutenant General von Knyphausen, the new uniforms are to be put on, and the proper appearance is recommended. The old uniforms are not to be sold, and the soldiers are to wear them every time when drawing provisions or wood. The soldiers are to be washed and combed at all times, and the quarters are to be assiduously smoked and cleaned. While doing garrison duty, the soldiers are to be powdered, and in general must make a good appearance.

Mirbach Order Book

Extract of the Gracious Letter
of His Serene Highness
to Lieutenant General von Knyphausen
Dated Wiessenstein, 22 September 1777

Extend my complete satisfaction to my soldiers for their exemplary conduct during the recent expedition into the Jerseys, and especially the good conduct of Lieutenant Colonel [Friedrich Ludwig] von Minnegerode and his battalion, who are to be informed of my satisfaction at muster. State my satisfaction to Lieutenant Colonel von Minnegerode personally, and that for leading the subordinates of his distinguished grenadier battalion as well and bravely in an affair into Jersey, he has earned the Orden pour la vertu Militaire. I find it necessary to repeat the need of caring for the sick, and a strict investigation into the previous and perhaps still existing neglect by company chiefs and hospital attendants. All those sick individuals left behind here by the regiments, will no longer be listed as absent, but dropped completely, and only those in America, present or sick, will be noted on the lists.

For the sake of maintaining good order, as well as reducing the excesses and plundering which is still being reported, and has not entirely ceased, the lieutenant general will issue the strictest orders against that, and the guilty persons are to be severely punished. Also, to insure the best order and discipline in the regiments on the march, no straggling will be tolerated, but the troops will be kept together, and all confusion prevented. The corps will be diligently drilled while in winter quarters.

Extract, Philadelphia, 9 February 1778
Promotions and Transfers

1) Major General Heldring retired on pension

Promoted to Major General

1) Colonel von Buelow to commandant at Rinteln, and chief of the previously Heldring Garrison Regiment

2) Colonel von Huyn

To Lieutenant Colonel

1) Major von Cruse at Schlotheim

To Major

1) Ridingmaster Roux with the Gendarmes

2) Ridingmaster von Gilsa of the Carabinier Regiment

3) Captain Biedenkapp of the Leib Dragoon Regiment of the Heister Regiment

Transferred

1) Lieutenant Colonel von Witternus from Schlothiem to the Carabiniers

The distinguished regiments, battalion, are ordered herewith to be more attentive when provisions or rations are received in the future than in the past, on

Mirbach Order Book

transport ships as well as on land, by the English commissaries, so that

1) In case of embarking or debarking so that land and ships' provisions, or double rations, are not received and signed for on the day, and

2) That only two-thirds rations are received when aboard ships, and that full ships' rations are not receipted for, and in the first instance, for every double and excessive portion received, not two and one-half pence, the actual value is paid, but nine pence sterling, and in the second situation, two pence sterling instead of two and one-quarter pence for each ration, the corps is charged two pence sterling, which surplus can not be authorized by anyone but those officers or regimental quartermaster who have signed or authorized the same.

The 14th - General Schmidt orders that the sick be sent to the company hospitals.

The 15th - The colonel orders that the new uniforms be worn only on duty, or when the soldiers have leave in the city, so that the old uniforms are worn and the new ones saved.

The 16th, 17th, and 18th - Nothing.

The 19th - As the colonel is aware that the troops have not properly maintained their leather items, he orders that the officers give more attention to see that those items are kept polished and in good order.

The 20th and 21st - Nothing.

Mirbach Order Book

<u>The 22nd</u> - Butchers in the companies are to be given strict orders that no cattle are to be slaughtered until they have a receipt by Major [Emanuel Anshelm] von Wilmowsky, who will assign the cost of the meat after purchase, and so inform the companies. The 1st sergeants shall be responsible that nothing is done in opposition to this order.

<u>The 23rd, 24th, and 25th</u> - Nothing.

<u>The 26th</u> - As the offenders, non-commissioned officers and privates, have been seen by the colonel, shooting at birds and thus destroying gardens, as well as endangering the health of children, the same is strictly forbidden, and will be punished by running the gauntlet. The cartridges are to be strictly accounted for and checked at every future quarters inspection.

<u>The 27th</u> - Nothing.

<u>The 28th</u> - When the regiments have settled accounts with the soldiers, the uniform accessories deduction are to be sent to General Schmidt.

Regimental Order

As General Schmidt is greatly displeased with the carousing by the non-commissioned officers and privates, and the frequently resulting excesses, the colonel herewith informs all the companies that the general intends to give exemplary punishment to the first soldier causing a complaint. The already so often repeated order that no soldier go into the city unless

Mirbach Order Book

accompanied by a non-commissioned officer, except on market days, is strictly repeated, and the non-commissioned officer who allows one of his men to be out of his sight and does not return him to the company, will be arrested immediately, and severely punished. Because of the firing by non-commissioned officers and privates, which causes a waste of ammunition, the general has also given the strictest orders that the most severe punishment should curtail that in the future.

March

The 1st, 2nd, and 3rd - Nothing.

The 4th of March - When companies send sick individuals to the hospital in New York, the Hospital Administrator Gerland is to be informed on the previous day, as he is responsible for the rationing and providing the necessary space.

The 5th, 6th, 7th, and 8th - Nothing.

The 9th - The pickets and guards are to be aware of all suspicious persons, arrest them at once, and send them to the staff watch.

Copy of the gracious order of 10 May 1777

My Etc.,

1) The march of battalions, and on parade remains in all cases, at 75 full steps per minute, and this also when advancing or retreating, even when

Mirbach Order Book

deployed, when passing through, during, battalion wheeling, counter-marching, and crossing bridges, turning on an axis, or when, after breaking off from wheeling and again forming by files and reassembling. The only exemption being when the battalion, at parade march in columns, and the platoon wheels. The wheeling must be made at a cadence of 110 steps per minute, because this is the only way that the rear units need not halt, and can keep their intervals. Therefore, the officers must give commands, one quickly following after the other - Halt, wheel! Halt, dress! March! And no long interval shall be between commands. Platoon step remains at the old cadence, and the heel will be placed ahead of the toe of the other foot.

2) When assuming a prone position, the left hand will no longer be placed on the knee, but a hand's width above the knee, making the movement easier. The left knee will be bent slightly forward, which aids in standing up more quickly.

3) When the battalion or parade group marches away, the unit will wheel, and the officers will no longer command - Halt, dress!, but the commander alone will order - March!

4) When counter-marching, the officers are no longer to command but only the commander alone shall order - Counter-march! Right-about! March! Halt front!, March!

Mirbach Order Book

The 11th and 12th - Nothing.

The 13th - As complaints have been received again that the shooting has not ceased, and that even balls have been fired, the same is again to cease, for fear of punishment, by running the gauntlet.

The 14th - Nothing.

The 15th - The colonel trusts that during the present good weather, the officers will exert every effort to insure that the companies' clumsy individuals are drilled.

The 16th, 17th, and 18th - Nothing.

The 19th - The auditors are to send money from auctions to War Councilor Lorenz, and as soon as that is done, show the receipt to General Schmidt.

The 20th - The colonel orders that company commanders are to insure that every man must have and protect a pay book in which everything that he receives, that he owes and repays, just as it is used in peace time.

It has come to the colonel's attention that the non-commissioned officers and privates are constantly carousing and fill the bars, especially on Sundays, and are getting drunk. This results in the worst excesses. Therefore it is strictly ordered that the officers take notice of this, and especially inspect the quarters on Sundays, and control their troops.

The 21st, 22nd, and 23rd - Nothing.

The 24th - The commanding general has advised,

Mirbach Order Book

by Lieutenant General Clinton, that the usual forage money is to be paid for 165 days.

Order, Philadelphia, 6 March

In accordance with the gracious order of His Serene Highness, the Landgrave, the following is to be noted and put into effect in all the Hessian regiments, battalions, and corps.

    1) When closing to the left or right, the head [of the unit] should no longer look toward the wing toward which they are moving, but the entire battalion is to look toward the middle. During the closing to the right, the right foot will be moved smartly sideways and at the same time to the front, with the left foot moved across the right foot, and carried forward. During closing to the left, this will be done in the opposite manner. All possible care will be taken during this left and right closing to insure no shoulder moving too far ahead or behind, but will march with an aligned front, so that the upper body of each man will stay in the designated place where he was before the movement, thus maintaining a straight line, and the movement will not lead to the wrong place.

    2) The units will form, as soon as they complete the movement, three yards from one another.

    3) At the command - By platoons! Half steps will be taken, forty per minute, when moving forward

or backward, and no longer will the heel be placed in front of the toe.

4) When the rear unit of the battalion is to shoot when charging, it will no longer move to the left and right from both wings. The left wing, as the second half of the battalion, alone will take four steps sideways to the left, while the right wing remains in place. When the unit is to open [close seems more appropriate], again the left wing alone will move four steps to the right in order to once again close the hole.

5) During Hackenfeuer [?] the files which have moved inward must watch out for the squad leader of the third rank who, after completing the movement at the same time, must realign, fore and aft, and load.

6) When deploying, the company guide will halt at the front, a bit to one side, so that the interior files have extra time to move closer together.

Mirbach Order Book

<u>Rules, according to which funeral ceremonies will be conducted</u>

1) Flags and pennants will be carried with the staffs held high, but not so high that the staff rests under the arm, and with the right hand reversed, the left hand pressed flat against the body.

2) Officers of the Cavalry, when mounted, will carry their sword or saber, covered, under the left arm, and when on foot, with the left hand pressed against the body.

3) When the body passes at the funeral parlor, or is carried into the church, or into the cemetery, [individuals] will present arms and the death march will be played and beaten. The death march for the hautboists is the 38th Psalm, which will be alternately played, with the drum roll and two single taps on the tambourines after each pause of the music. The pipers of the grenadier companies play the song, with the tambourines in the same manner. I request this in the most heart-felt manner.

4) At the funeral of generals, the kettle drums and trumpets will be draped with a black cloth. For a chief, who is not a general, as well as for staff officers, captains, and subalterns, the kettle drums, trumpets, and drums will only be muffled.

Next, it is announced that as a result of the death of General of Infantry von Bose, governor of

Mirbach Order Book

Cassel, as well as the Guard Regiment, General von Bardeleben is confirmed commander, and colonel. On the other hand, Major General von Jungkenn is named colonel and commander of the 1st Battalion; Colonel von Donop is named lieutenant colonel, and Lieutenant Colonels von Stueckrad and von Rotzmann are named majors. Colonel von Horn is named commander of the Garrison Regiment von Balcke, and a company thereof is given to him.

The 25th of March - By order of Lieutenant General Clinton, a picket is to be sent to the East River by the Wissenbach Battalion, and a picket from the von Mirbach Regiment is to patrol the North River. The colonel therefore orders that the picket normally in the quarters will receive three more men from each company. This picket will man no post, but will patrol as soon as going on duty, from Major von Wilmowsky, to Major Baurmeister, to the Vacant Company, then to the Leib Company, and from the Leib Company to the Colonel's Company, on to the staff watch, and finally from the staff watch to the cannon foundry, and then each time return. The patrol will be sent out every hour, and the non-commissioned officers will be informed that, if the patrols do not move out on time, they will be demoted, so that an example will be made of the first one who fails to follow orders. An officer will spend the night in the hut in front of the

Mirbach Order Book

Leib Company. The officers do not need to report to the staff except under special circumstances.

The picket non-commissioned officer will report to the company officer every day to receive the necessary instructions which apply, so that they are attentive on their posts to everything which occurs, challenge everyone who seems suspicious, and take them to the staff watch, or, if in boats, fire at them.

The 26th, 27th, and 28th - Nothing.

The 29th - As the greatest complaint has been received that the defenses which have been newly constructed are being torn down, and footpaths made, this is strictly forbidden, and any person caught will be punished severely to prevent the recurrence.

The 30th - Nothing.

The 31st - By order of General von Mirbach, paydays in the future will be held every five days, with the first being held tomorrow.

April

The 1st - Nothing.

The 2nd - The colonel orders that in every quarters location during the day, a post will be established on the North River, which can see over everything. It is understood that those three men who are on that post during the day will no longer be assigned to the usual picket, but will be taken therefrom. The non-commissioned officer of the picket will be responsible for inspecting the post during the day.

The 3rd of April - The colonel orders all company commanders to complete their accounts to the end of March, with Major Baurmeister's Company completed on the 23rd of the month, followed by the vacant company and the Colonel's Company. The Leib Company will make their accounting with the general himself.

At the same time, all the companies will account with the regimental quartermaster for the recruits and uniform accessories for 1777, and for the uniform accessories for the first quarter of 1778. If they do not require this money, instead of cash, they will receive a receipt or the surplus, and the regimental quartermaster will deposit the money with War Councilor Lorenz, along with the surplus company funds.

At nine o'clock in the morning, on the 6th of this month, if the weather is good, the companies will march out to an open place near their quarters to drill. The old uniforms will be worn. The companies are to arrange by the week, to send their weapons to the gunsmith for repairs.

The 4th and 5th - Nothing.

The 6th - At eight-thirty in the morning weapons will be issued. The companies will arrange their moving out so that drill will commence precisely at nine o'clock. The troops are to have their hair trimmed, and above all, the men are to give the best possible appearance.

The 7th - The following promotions are announced:

1) Colonel von Diemar is promoted to major general and the vacant Heister Dragoon Regiment is to be given to him.

2) Colonel Klambeck of the Garrison Artillery is promoted to major general, as is Colonel von Gohr of the Field Artillery.

3) Major Wagenhols, who has been on pension, is placed in this same rank with the 2nd Battalion of the Stein Garrison Regiment.

The 8th and 9th - Nothing.

The 10th - The colonel orders that the staff watch assemble at one o'clock in the future, so that fewer people miss drill.

Company commanders are to weigh some of the bread when it is received.

The 11th - A large number of rebels escaped from the sugar house prison during the night, two of whom were captured by Major von Wilmowsky's Company, which meets with General [James] Robertson's approval, and he has ordered that a reward be paid to the troops who made the arrest. All the pickets and guards will be alert to watch for suspicious persons, in order to perhaps catch some more of these deserters.

The 12th, 13th, 14th, 15th, 16th, and 17th - Nothing.

The 18th - The proper conduct of the troops is to be observed at all times. The colonel orders that in the morning and throughout the day, they are to be frequently inspected in their quarters, in order to prevent all fighting and other excesses. Every non-commissioned officer is responsible for the troops quartered in his house.

The 19th - The colonel again orders most strictly, that neither soldiers nor non-commissioned officers be given leave to go into the city today, or tomorrow, and a non-commissioned officer from each company is to be ordered to check the bars at the earliest opportunity to prevent fighting and drunkenness.

The 20th - Tomorrow at eight o'clock all the carpenters and one man per company are to report to Lieutenant Keyser, where they will be trained with the cannons. The men now on that detail are not relieved.

The 21st - Nothing.

The 22nd - On orders of General Schmidt those troops having credits are to be paid, but not before they receive further orders, and are so notified by the chiefs and commanders, so that the pay books of those soldiers can be brought up to date, as of this time. General Schmidt will be present when the troops are asked if they have received all [that is due nine o'clock. The troops are to have their hair trimmed, and above all, the men are to give the best possible appearance.

The 7th - The following promotions are announced:

1) Colonel von Diemar is promoted to major general and the vacant Heister Dragoon Regiment is to be given to him.

2) Colonel Klambeck of the Garrison Artillery is promoted to major general, as is Colonel von Gohr of the Field Artillery.

3) Major Wagenhols, who has been on pension, is placed in this same rank with the 2nd Battalion of the Stein Garrison Regiment.

The 8th and 9th - Nothing.

The 10th - The colonel orders that the staff watch assemble at one o'clock in the future, so that fewer people miss drill.

Company commanders are to weigh some of the bread when it is received.

The 11th - A large number of rebels escaped from the sugar house prison during the night, two of whom were captured by Major von Wilmowsky's Company, which meets with General [James] Robertson's approval, and he has ordered that a reward be paid to the troops who made the arrest. All the pickets and guards will be alert to watch for suspicious persons,

Mirbach Order Book

in order to perhaps catch some more of these deserters.

The 12th, 13th, 14th, 15th, 16th, and 17th - Nothing.

The 18th - The proper conduct of the troops is to be observed at all times. The colonel orders that in the morning and throughout the day, they are to be frequently inspected in their quarters, in order to prevent all fighting and other excesses. Every non-commissioned officer is responsible for the troops quartered in his house.

The 19th - The colonel again orders most strictly, that neither soldiers nor non-commissioned officers be given leave to go into the city today, or tomorrow, and a non-commissioned officer from each company is to be ordered to check the bars at the earliest opportunity to prevent fighting and drunkenness.

The 20th - Tomorrow at eight o'clock all the carpenters and one man per company are to report to Lieutenant Keyser, where they will be trained with the cannons. The men now on that detail are not relieved.

The 21st - Nothing.

The 22nd - On orders of General Schmidt those troops having credits are to be paid, but not before they receive further orders, and are so notified by the chiefs and commanders, so that the pay books of those soldiers can be brought up to date, as of this time. General Schmidt will be present when the troops are asked if they have received all [that is due

Mirbach Order Book

them].

The 23rd, 24th, and 25th - Nothing.

The 26th - As of tomorrow the new uniforms will be worn at drill, but at the same time it is strictly ordered that they be clean and in the best condition. It will also be forbidden for the soldiers to wet the white items when coloring them, as this causes them to turn yellow.

The 27th - Every Wednesday and Saturday afternoon, the clumsy soldiers who have not mastered the drill will be trained by a company officer,

The colonel orders that all soldiers, except those on duty or at drill, are forbidden to wear the new uniform, and are strictly cautioned to prevent damage to the same.

War Councilor Lorenz requests that on the special order of His Serene Highness, the field requisition lists submitted and attested to are to be signed by the officers of the company in the proper manner, and furthermore, that each has the signatures and seals thereon.

If the listed items, due to special circumstances, have truly been lost and can not be recovered, this should be attested on our word of honor.

The 28th, 29th, and 30th - Nothing.

Mirbach Order Book

May

The 1st, 2nd, and 3rd - Nothing.

The 4th - Three cannon shots are the signal for the Hessian regiments to go to their alarm places. Major General Valentine Jones is to succeed General Robertson as commandant of New York. General Robertson has been ordered to take over the command of the troops on Rhode Island and therefore must be ready to go there.

General Schmidt orders that when firing exercises are conducted, it must be reported each time, and is to be held between nine and ten o'clock.

The 5th - General Schmidt orders the regiment to be prepared for drill tomorrow morning at eight o'clock, and each man is to take ten cartridges with him. The general will give verbal orders as to where the firing is to be conducted.

The 6th and 7th - Nothing.

The 8th - General Schmidt orders that today and tomorrow the troops with credits are to be paid.

The 9th and 10th - Nothing.

The 11th - Tomorrow all the soldiers are to take their pay books with them to the drill ground.

The 12th and 13th - Nothing.

The 14th - Order of His Serene Highness, dated Wabern, 29 May 1776.

In the future, the battalion will be formed in the following manner:

Mirbach Order Book

When the battalion falls in, the officers and non-commissioned officers will move to the front center of their companies, the first according to their seniority, the latter according to height, the drummers of the Leib Company on the right wing; those of the left company on the left wing of the same. Those of the 2nd and 4th companies ahead of their right wing; and those of the middle company with the regimental drummer in front of the right flank of the second platoon. To their right stand the hautboists. The flags are carried before the second platoon of the Leib Company.

When the weapons are inspected, the captains and commanders of the staff companies will all order, at the same time - Attention! Present arms! Left [shoulder] arms! etc. The five squad leaders of the companies turn to each other and snatch [the weapons] at the same time. After being shouldered, each company orders - Form files! The captains and commanders of the companies will form the files in two platoons, and inspect the files. <u>NB</u> - the adjutant must have received the strength reports for the companies from the first sergeants prior to this time, so that when they have an open file, they can help one another, and on the command - Form arms! the open files of all the companies can be completed.

After the files are inspected, the captains or commanders of the companies order - Officers and non-commissioned officers post! On this command, the captain or senior officer moves to the front of the file, second from the right, the next senior officers before the left wing, and the youngest before the second file. They arrange themselves ahead of the companies in such a manner that they are an equal distance from one another and take positions equally spaced. The non-commissioned officers are placed not according to seniority, but according to height, with the shortest at the rear of the platoon, whether sergeants or free corporals. With the wing companies, the non-commissioned officer are also assigned on the flanks of the second and third ranks.

When the battalion marches away, those on the left flank move up and close behind the last platoon, but as soon as the front is formed, they return again to the second and third ranks. Thereupon, the chief or commander orders the battalion - Form the battalion! The two most junior officers who previously were standing with their companies form according to their height on this command. At the left wing company, the senior officer moves ahead of the second file on that wing, and the third senior before the second platoon. Some of the tallest soldiers of the company arrange themselves on the left and right flank also on the command - Form the battalion! according to height. The commander orders - Present arms! and the flag moves ahead of the Leib Company on the

Mirbach Order Book

right wing of the sixth platoon, ahead of the drummers standing there.

The major is no longer to ride around the battalion in order to inspect the files, but commands - Battalion, load! The 1st sergeants of all the companies on this command proceed behind the sixth platoon, and the drummers standing at the front move to the flank, as usual. When the platoons move forward, the officers enter the battalion, the senior on the flank, and the next senior, to the second platoon of the company. In the left wing companies, however, the senior moves to the left and the next senior to the right flank, and the third senior into the middle of the company. All other officers fall in behind the platoon. The flags and four 1st sergeants move between the fifth and sixth platoons. The six flag files, as usual, will be separated by a non-commissioned officer of the fifth platoon, and the fifth 1st sergeant. Both left flank companies will be arranged as previously on the left.

After the drill, companies will not be reformed. The guard will not be doubled. Instead the command will be given - Guards, fall out! Those individuals will move to form in the front center. The company will close up the files, and then form into four platoons. When a battalion, which is formed in this new manner, must march about with spaces between platoons, the following will be observed. The captains or senior officers of all companies will lead the first platoon; the next senior, the second platoon. The two junior officers march behind the captain and ahead of the first platoon, according to their height.

In the left flank companies, the senior officer moves to the side. The next senior leads the first platoon, and the third senior the second platoon. The flags march at the head of the sixth platoon, with the two most junior officers beside them on the left and right flanks, according to their height. Should one of those officers be absent, another will be sent from the next company. The 1st sergeants remain behind the flag platoon during the marching activity. So as to prevent too many non-commissioned officers following the sixth platoon during the marching, the non-commissioned officers will be used to cover the flanks. The three drummers march ahead of the first platoon; those of the middle-most company, however, ahead of the second platoon, behind the flags. Three drummers of the left flank companies however, behind the tenth platoon.

The 15th - The old uniforms can now be used to make gloves for the coming winter.

The 16th - The missing cartridges must be turned in, figured at forty rounds per man.

The 17th - At six o'clock tomorrow the companies are to be at their quarters ready to move out on the shortest notice. All leaving of the quarters is therefore forbidden.

Mirbach Order Book

<u>The 18th and 19th</u> - Nothing.

<u>The 20th</u> - General Schmidt orders that the Hessian von Mirbach Regiment provide one officer, one non-commissioned officer, and eighteen privates for a command at Turtle Bay, which post the Wissenbach Regiment has provided.

General Tryon is to command the troops on Long Island in the future.

<u>The 21st and 22nd</u> - Nothing.

<u>The 23rd</u> - General Schmidt orders that the content of the accompanying correspondence from His Excellency Lieutenant General von Knyphausen be obeyed exactly.

At the beginning of the coming month the linen trousers are to be worn.

(Copy) - Honorable Sir,

Especially the respected major general,

By the timely arrival of your most recent letter, I have been assured of the events of the thirteenth and fifteenth of the previous month.

No doubt, in accordance with my letter of 31 March, the companies have settled accounts with the soldiers to the end of 1777, and paid the amounts owed. Therefore, try, according to the following plan, to complete an extract of the amounts paid to all the soldiers there, and submit it to me.

This order is also distributed so that the missing and damaged field requisition lists can be prepared, and submitted as soon as possible to War Councilor Lorenz, so that the repairs and replacements of those items can be provided for the effective men. The limited supply of new items which are available will be distributed proportionately to the regiments in New York and [New] Scotland [Nova Scotia]. The surplus costs must be assumed by the companies, however, until the matter is resolved by His Serene Highness. The same situation applies to the acquisition of linen trousers for the soldiers.

With, etc.
Philadelphia, 11 May 1778
Knyphausen

(Copy)

My Dear Major General von Mirbach,

Lieutenant Carl von Ehrenstein, previously in Prussian service, has been assigned to your regiment as an ensign as of 20 October 1777. He leaves here tomorrow with the departing jaegers and the recruit transport. He will report with his commissioning papers.

I remain with esteem for the good affections of the major general,

Friedrich, Landgrave of Hesse
Cassel, 13 November 1777

- - - - - - -

<u>The 24th</u> - Nothing.

<u>The 25th</u> - The extract requested by Lieutenant

General von Knyphausen is to be completed and submitted as soon as possible.

The 1st Battalion of the 71st Regiment is to march into camp on the coming Thursday at McGowan's line near the John's house, and Fanning's Corps, on the same day, goes to Newtown on Long Island.

The Hessian detachment near McGowan's house is to march tomorrow, after the arrival of the 71st Regiment, back into the city, but will leave behind a captain, two officers, and 100 privates in the redoubt on the right hand, as well as one captain, one officer, and fifty men at Harlem, as Colonel Robinson will be leaving that post. The von Wissenbach Regiment is to be prepared to march on the shortest notice. Therefore General Schmidt orders that the von Mirbach Regiment occupy Marston's Wharf with a detachment consisting of one non-commissioned officer and nine men, relieving the von Wissenbach, which now occupies it, and reducing their internal duties.

The 26th - The von Wissenbach Regiment is to march tomorrow to Fort Knyphausen.

The 27th - No forage is to be received as of the 31st of this month according to the regulations from the commanding general.

The 28th - Nothing.

The 29th - The colonel orders that when the regiment receives an order to march, the officers and middle staff personnel reduce their equipment and

Mirbach Order Book

send everything possible to the baggage house.

The companies are to report how many of the fifteen tent axes they are short, tomorrow.

Ensign von Ehrenstein is temporarily assigned to the vacant company.

The 30th - As of today, not more than an eighth of a cord of wood will be carried in a canoe.

The 31st - As of tomorrow the linen trousers will be worn. As the repair costs and completing the field requisitioning may be too expensive for the companies, it is Lieutenant General von Knyphausen's intention that the war chest advance the payment which remains a burden on them, until the matter is resolved by His Highness.

June

The 1st - The army is informed that General Clinton has assumed command, and General Howe is returning [to England].

Forage money is to be paid for 200 days. No officer is to receive a double amount.

The 2nd - As Thursday is the King's birthday, General Schmidt orders the soldiers who will be in the city to be well and properly dressed.

The 3rd - Nothing.

The 4th - When three cannon shots and three rockets are fired from the redoubt at McGowan's, the von Mirbach Regiment will take up arms and form with a front along the North River, on the closest road

Mirbach Order Book

to Bloomingdale, three miles from New York. The regiment will send an experienced officer to headquarters for additional orders. This officer is not to cause an alarm in New York.

The colonel orders that the new woolen trousers be delivered to the soldiers, and they are to be taken care of in a proper manner.

The 5th and 6th - Nothing.

The 7th - The regiment is herewith notified that Lieutenant Colonel [Karl Christian] von Romrod of the Landgrave Regiment has been transferred as colonel and commandant of this regiment. Also, Ensigns [Georg Bernhard] Kersting and [Rudolf Wilhelm] Duncker of the von Huyn Regiment, as second lieutenants, and Ensign [Martin Ludwig] Wisker, in grade, have been transferred to this regiment.

As Colonel von Romrod wishes to get acquainted with all the officers, they are ordered to assemble every morning at nine o'clock in Colonel von Borck's quarters.

The 8th - The regiment is notified that Lieutenant Kersting replaces Lieutenant [Dietrich] von Gottschall, who died of his wounds, in the Grenadier Company. Lieutenant Duncker is assigned to Colonel von Romrod's Company, and Ensign Wisker is temporarily assigned to the Leib Company.

The 9th - On orders of the colonel, the damaged

Mirbach Order Book

tents are to be measured by a tailor in the presence of a captain, an officer, and the regimental quarter-master, and the results submitted to War Councilor Lorenz.

The 10th, 11th, and 12th - Nothing.

The 13th - The companies are to have their equipment, which is to be sent to the baggage house, ready to be shipped there on the shortest notice. Each company must have the cover, or whatever else contains the baggage, marked with the company number, and a list of the contents.

They must leave out those items which they will need available, such as soles, shoes, etc., so as not to have to send to the city so often. The non-commissioned officer, on command with the baggage, has the key to the staff and all other baggage, and no one else is to be allowed to take anything out.

The 14th - The heavy baggage is to be sent to the city at daybreak tomorrow.

The 15th - No safeguard is to be given except on order of the commanding general. It shall be submitted, why it was submitted, and on whose orders.

The 16th - General Schmidt has found that the order given concerning wood has not been followed exactly. Therefore he orders the regimental commanders to give strict adherence that the same is observed, and under no pretext is wood to be made for the tents except what the general only directs his

Mirbach Order Book

regimental commanders to retain. Above all, they are to report every incident which is contrary to duty and the direct order. The colonel orders that no horse and wagon serve except for the usual acquisition, and otherwise nothing else shall be done except on orders of the staff.

One shovel and axe will be delivered per company today. Each company which is short of these after delivery shall pay for each item.

The 17th - Detached individuals on duty with the baggage are to be relieved every four weeks until further notice, and receive pay and provisions from the company. When it is necessary for the companies to get something from the baggage, which can not be imagined during the first four weeks, three days in the week, Monday, Thursday, and Saturday at eight o'clock are designated. Lieutenant [Johann Bartholomai] Becker of the Buenau Regiment has the key to the baggage house, and the non-commissioned officer who is to pick up the baggage must report to him. Also, on the coming Friday morning, the companies are to submit to me a list of what they have by way of sacks, kegs, bales, etc., as well as the company name and number, in the baggage house. It will be necessary that officers who wish to have additional items sent to their baggage, also submit lists of that not found on the previous list. These lists will be forwarded for Lieutenant Becker's information.

Mirbach Order Book

<u>The 18th</u> - The artillery of each regiment will be included in the provision's list in an appended report.

It is also announced that the von Mirbach Regiment will not camp before the house.

The colonel orders that in the future anyone arrested, regardless of whom it might be, will be sent initially to the staff watch and reported to the same.

<u>The 19th</u> - Nothing.

<u>The 20th</u> - His Serene Highness has announced the following in the regiment:

The previously Major [Hans Moritz] von Biesenrodt is promoted to lieutenant colonel and awarded the von Scheick Company.

Captain [Johann Wilhelm] Endemann of the regiment is promoted to major of the Woellwarth Regiment.

Captain [Friedrich Andreas] Schotten is recalled to Hesse.

1st Lieutenant [Johann Ludwig] Rodemann and 2nd Lieutenant [Karl Henrich] von Toll are both promoted to staff captain.

2nd Lieutenants [Friedrich August] von Broescke and [Johann Konrad] Schraidt are promoted to 1st lieutenant, the first to have the pay as of 1 March, the latter as of 1 October.

Both Free Corporals [Friedrich] Lange and [Friedrich Wilhelm] Feyare promoted to ensign, the first to have the pay as of 1 February, the latter, as of

Mirbach Order Book

1 October.

Lieutenant [Ferdinand] Unger of the Wuerttemberg service has been transferred to this regiment as a supernumerary.

Ensign [Karl Wilhelm] von Bilsingsloewen is transferred to the Grenadier Company.

Lieutenant [Karl Friedrich] Rueffer is appointed adjutant.

The following officers are transferred to the companies indicated:

1) Grenadier Company - Captain [Louis Marie de] Mallet, 1st Lieutenant Broescke, and 2nd Lieutenants von Bilsingsloewen and Kersting

2) The Leib Company - Captain [David] Reichhold, 2nd Lieutenants [Ludwig Wilhelm August] von Boyneburgh and [Hieronymus] Berner, and Ensign Unger (supernumerary)

3) Colonel von Romrod - Captain [Johann Melchior] Rothe, 2nd Lieutenant Duncker, and Ensign Lange

4) Lieutenant Colonel von Biesenrodt - Captain von Toll, 2nd Lieutenant [Hans Friedrich] von Biesenrodt, and Ensign [Karl] von Ehrenstein

5) Major von Wilmowsky - 1st Lieutenant Schraidt, 2nd Lieutenant [Johann Georg] Wissenmueller, and Ensign Fey

6) Major Barmiest - Captain Rodemann, 2nd Lieutenant [Erhard] von Drach, and Ensign Wisker

Mirbach Order Book

Extract of the gracious letter of His Highness to Lieutenant General von Knyuphausen, Cassel, 3 December 1777

My feelings can easily be understood by the lieutenant general as to how pleased the news of the success achieved by the royal troops and a portion of my troops, which were present, made me, although the large losses suffered by so many good officers and men have created a deep feeling of sorrow. Nevertheless, the lieutenant general is to convey my complete satisfaction for the brave conduct displayed during this opportunity by the von Linsing and Minnigerode Grenadier Battalions, as well as the von Mirbach Regiment.

In order to demonstrate my satisfaction in a special manner, I send herewith:

1) The Orden pour la vertu Militaire for Lieutenant Colonel von Wurmb of the Jaeger Corps for his good dispositions and demonstrated bravery on 3 September, 4 October, and various other times.

2) For Captain [Karl August] von Wrede and

3) For Captain [Johannes] Ewald, both of the Jaeger Corps, for their demonstrated bravery also, and as witness thereof, include the decoration for them also.

4) Furthermore, the Orden is sent for the present Major [Philipp] von Wurmb of the Prince

Mirbach Order Book

Charles Regiment, and

    5) For 1st Lieutenant Friedrich Henrich von Groening of the Leib Infantry Regiment for their conduct in recapturing from enemy hands the redoubt on Providence Island on 11 October, which the lieutenant general confirmed, and

    6) For the current Major [Ludwig Friedrich von] Stamford of the Leib Infantry Regiment, for the brave defense against the enemy's frequent attacks on the same redoubt on the twelfth of last month. Further, on the recommendation of the lieutenant general, Sergeant [Alexander Wilhelm] Bickel of the Jaeger Corps is promoted to 2nd lieutenant, due to his demonstrated bravery at the affair at Brandywine Hill.

As the lieutenant colonels who have been promoted to colonel have had their dates of rank reserved also as captains, so the dates of rank are also reserved in their present promotions and they may anticipate receipt of their patents. As with other lieutenant colonels and majors who have been granted a date of rank, their dates of rank will be in accordance with their promotions.

<u>Promotions and Transfers</u>

    Colonel Block of the von Mirbach Regiment is retired.

    Lieutenant Colonel Leopold is promoted to Colonel in the Engineers.

Mirbach Order Book

Lieutenant Colonel von Romrod is promoted to colonel and commander of the von Mirbach Regiment.

Lieutenant Colonel von Keydel is promoted to colonel in the Guard Regiment.

Lieutenant Colonel [Johann Friedrich] von Cochenhausen is promoted to colonel in the Hereditary Prince Regiment.

Lieutenant Colonel von Minnigerode is promoted to colonel in the Knyphausen Regiment.

Major [Kasper Friedrich] von Hanstein is promoted to lieutenant colonel in the Landgraf Regiment.

Major Eitel is promoted to lieutenant colonel in the Artillery.

Major von Biesenrodt is promoted to lieutenant colonel in the Mirbach Regiment.

Captain von Wurmb is promoted to major in the Prince Charles Regiment.

Captain von Stamford is promoted to major in the Leib Regiment.

Captain [Georg Henrich] Pauli is promoted to major in the Artillery.

Captain Rodemann is promoted to major in the 1st Battalion of the Wissenbach Regiment.

Dated, Cassel, 16 February 1778

Lieutenant Colonel von Wurmb is named commander of the Jaeger Corps, and Major von

Wurmb of the Prince Charles Regiment is transferred to the Jaeger Corps.

Because of having received testimony from the lieutenant general concerning Ensign [Wilhelm Johann Ernst] Freyenhagen of the Donop Regiment repelling an attack on the Jaeger Corps picket at the ferry on 25 November, I wish to express my satisfaction and therefore have promoted him to second lieutenant in the Donop Regiment.

<u>Promotions and Transfers</u>
Major von Stahl is promoted to lieutenant colonel in the Leib Dragoon Regiment.

Major von Malsburg is promoted to lieutenant colonel in the Light Horse.

Riding Master [Captain] von Stein is promoted to major in the Carabiniers.

Captain von Trott is promoted to major in the Leib Dragoon Regiment.

Colonel [Franz Karl Erdmann] von Seitz is awarded the vacant Stein Garrison Regiment.

Major [Ludwig] von Schallern of the Wilcke Regiment is transferred to the Seitz Regiment.

Lieutenant Colonel von Schreyvogel is assigned to the Balcke Regiment.

Dated, Cassel, 16 February 1778
His highness does not know if the regiments have

Mirbach Order Book

flag bearers who are qualified for commissioning as officers, and who have attained the required age. He therefore wishes that those who are qualified be immediately recommended whenever a vacancy occurs.

von Jungkenn

Extract of the gracious letter of His Serene Highness
Dated, 16 February 1778

Because of the many men not from Hesse, who are in the Jaeger Corps, Lieutenant Colonel von Wurmb is ordered to double his attention, and to maintain the strictest discipline in the hope of reducing excesses, and making the men into good soldiers. Above all, the battalion and company chiefs or commanders are ordered, to do the same, because of the many men not from Hesse, as learned during the recent example in the last war, when the Austrian and especially the Prussian armies, had to recruit men from all the regions and nations to fill their vacancies.

Extract of the gracious letter of His Serene Highness
To Lieutenant General von Knyphausen
Dated 31 December 1777

It is with a constant and continuous interest that I receive reports that my orders concerning the conduct and care of the sick encountered there [in America] be strictly and exactly adhered to and have the desired result shown to the newly wounded and sick. Therefore I repeat my earnest orders and recommend that they be strictly adhered to.

It has often been the case that one or another officer, because of poor health was completely unfit to serve during a campaign, and has been called back [to Europe]. This has been reported to General Howe by the lieutenant general so that the arrangements can be made for them to return on a departing warship or frigate when the opportunity arose. Nevertheless, the lieutenant general has to determine if the individual is incapable of serving in the field, before the report of the situation can be sent to me, as otherwise no one from the corps [in America] will be called back.

Captain Endemann of the Mirbach Regiment is herewith promoted to major in the Woellwarth Regiment because he is a good and capable officer, and such is needed in that regiment.

Dated, 16 February 1778

Captain Schlotten of the Mirbach Regiment may return here from America at the earliest opportunity as he wishes to settle into civilian life.

All other officers who are ordered back to Hesse are to take note that they are never to travel on a packet boat, but at all times are to sail on a war or transport ship. The vacancy in the Prince Charles Regiment has already been filled by Ensign [Leopold Amandus von] Baillivy, and he will depart from here with the recruit shipment during the coming month of March.

By the last report received from General Schmidt, I learned of the expedition against Forts Clinton, Montgomery, and Constitution, which pleased me, as Generals Howe and Clinton praised the noteworthy conduct of the Truembach Regiment.

Captain [Friedrich] Platte, previously of the Stein Regiment, is promoted to major, and replaces Major [Christian Philipp] Mell of the Buenau Regiment, who is returning here. Captain Platte's patent is being sent with the order to Colonel von Seitz with the order to transfer him to the Buenau Regiment. Recently Lieutenant General [Johann Ludwig Ferdinand] von Stein zu Barchfeld died. The garrison regiment which was previously his has been conferred on Colonel von Seitz, and the patent is being sent to him. Major von Schallern is being transferred to the, from now on, von Seitz Regiment from the Wilcke Regiment, and will proceed to America with the next recruit shipment.

As reports have been received that both the Wissenbach and von Seitz Regiments are not in the best condition, the lieutenant general is ordered to give his best care and attention to them. I especially hope that due to the existing illness, which the staff officers suffer, that there is no lack of good conduct and diligent drill. If such should seem to be the case, I await the report from the lieutenant general.

Mirbach Order Book

<u>The 22nd</u> - As Lieutenant Duncker is to be transferred to the Grenadier Company, he is to be prepared to do so on the shortest notice. In his place, on the other hand, Bilsingsloewen is to be transferred to Colonel Romrod's Company.

<u>The 23rd and 24th</u> - Nothing.

<u>The 25th</u> - To Colonel von Borck, Sir, I send herewith, (Copy attached) on the orders of the Hessian Board of War's published directive, those who sit as members of a court-martial concerning life, death, or honor, are to be sworn according to the copy of the accompanying oath, in order to insure that this gracious order in future cases will be followed by the von Mirbach Regiment.

Philadelphia, 21 December 1777
Knyphausen

(Copy)

Sir, steadfast and true, my dear lieutenant general,

In accordance with His Serene Highness' decree concerning the oath for individuals assigned to courts-martial being retaken, it is ordered for the courts that sit on a court-martial dealing with life, death, or honor. Therefore, the lieutenant general has been ordered to make this known to all regiments there, and to insure that in future cases, this be strictly adhered to. Herewith we remain in service to him in friendship.

Mirbach Order Book

Cassel, 26 June 1777   Issued by the Board of War
                        Bar   Wangermann
                        Schramm   Engelhard

(Copy)

I, the president, and we, the assessors of the Board of War, praise and swear to God the Omnipotent, by this designated oath, that in the present case, concerning an inquiry about (person named), according to the Articles of War, will judge based on the impartial right, and our decision will not be made either from friendship, enmity, favor, gift, present, or donation, or other inducement, so help us God, in the name of Jesus Christ, our Savior.

The 26th - Soldiers, attendants, attendants, and other persons doing duty in the hospital are to draw provisions from the hospital only. From the day they are assigned there, they are to be stricken from the provisions' roll.

The 27th - The colonel orders that the company commander give strict attention that the linen trousers not be worn for other than duty.

Extract and gracious and generous announcement from the Hessian General Board of War and
War Councilor Lorenz
Dated, Cassel, 16 March 1778

Mirbach Order Book

In order to fill vacancies in the regiments and corps we must inform War Councilor Lorenz that according to the rule and the previous agreement, the corps must be complete upon the opening of the campaign, including the vacancies of company chiefs, which must be filled without fail. Also, should these replacements be readily available, the wages are to be drawn from the English Crown. As no one can tell if the number of recruits being sent is large enough to replace the losses, War Councilor Lorenz has stopped the pay for all vacancies which the companies have at the start of the campaign, or can muster at this time. Still the pay for such vacancies, if allowed to remain after the mustering or start of the campaign, must be figured anew. Here it is necessary to be extremely careful in order to be sure in every case.

Extract, New York, 23 June 1778

The 28th - The colonel orders that during pay formation tomorrow, the companies inform the men of the sincere satisfaction His Serene Highness, the Landgrave, received from the attack on Fort Red Bank. Therefore the colonel hopes that during every future opportunity that everyone, as mentioned above, be so informed, so that thereby the regiments can retain the well-earned praise and always keep it.

The 29th - Nothing.

The 30th - The guard of honor for the commis-

Mirbach Order Book

sioners, one captain, one lieutenant, one ensign, and fifty men will receive them at Trinity Church; the duty guard for them will consist of one subaltern and twenty men.

July

The 1st, 2nd and 3rd - Nothing.

The 4th - The colonel orders those officers who have not yet moved into company quarters, where assigned, to do so without fail by this coming Monday. Also, a different officer will inspect the quarters daily and assure everything is in order.

The von Mirbach Regiment is to be prepared to enter camp on the shortest notice.

The 5th - As the colonel has been informed that despite the previous orders, soldiers go into the city almost everyday, unaccompanied by non-commissioned officers, he strictly orders that the commander order the non-commissioned officers in the quarters not to grant leave to any individual without the prior approval of the company commander, and the first one to do so will be severely punished. Letters addressed to General von Jungkenn are to be forwarded to War Councilor Lorenz each time, so that they are delivered to the packet boat which insures the earliest delivery to the general.

The 6th - All the Hessian regiments are to assemble on New York Island.

The 7th and 8th - Nothing.

Mirbach Order Book

The 9th - The Mirbach Regiment is to leave the cantonment quarters at first light tomorrow and enter camp where the 38th Regiment has been stationed previously. The colonel therefore orders that the regiment fall out at its quarters at precisely five o'clock in the morning. The Leib Company with the flags and the Colonel's Company are to await the staff before Captain Rothe's quarters.

Quartermaster sergeants and guards are to assemble at the same time, at the quarters of the regimental quartermaster in order to mark out [the company areas.]

All non-commissioned officers who are on picket duty this evening will serve either at the place assigned, or at the quarters of the company commanders, so as to be able to deliver every place over to the relieving English in the best manner.

The 10th - Until the Grenadiers and the Light Infantry Battalions are reformed, Major Medlands is to take command of those companies, whose battalions are not present.

Regimental Order

The going out by the soldiers is in no way permitted, and if it is necessary for them to obtain something, a non-commissioned officer is to accompany them. From officers to privates, no one is allowed into the city, or anywhere else, and those who obtain permission must be back at the regiment by

Mirbach Order Book

retreat. After retreat, no one is to have leave. When the password is announced at five o'clock in the afternoon, all officers and non-commissioned officers not on duty, must be present. When an individual is to run a gauntlet of switches, no damage is to be done to the trees surrounding the camp. At various and indeterminate times during the day, roll call is to be held. Anyone who is absent will be severely punished, as no soldier is permitted outside the tents without the previous permission of his commander.

<u>The 11th</u> - Nothing.

<u>The 12th</u> - Every morning before daybreak the regiment is to be alert, so as to immediately respond to the first alert.

<u>The 13th</u> - When the 57th Regiment marches, the Hessians must assume the watch.

The password will be given out at six o'clock in the evening. All officers, non-commissioned officers and even artillery officers, must be present. At evening roll call, the officers must be present at the company. The 1st sergeant will then report to them and also to the adjutant, who will then report to the staff. During review the commands - Shoulder arms! and Order arms! will no longer be employed, but the weapons will be taken to the feet, and on the shoulder at a regular cadence as the units advance. By tattoo everyone who has had leave, is to be at the regiment, whether officers, non-commissioned officers, or

Mirbach Order Book

privates.

The 14th - Nothing.

The 15th - Early tomorrow morning a detachment of one officer, four non-commissioned officers, one drummer, and forty privates will be provided for escorting the prisoners. This detachment is to be provided with one day's rations, and be at the North Church at three o'clock in the morning, where the officer will receive his instructions.

The 16th - On orders of his excellence, the general-in-chief, a non-commissioned officer and sixteen men [or ten - figure not clear] will be provided at his home in the country, one and one half English miles from the city.

The 17th - Nothing.

The 18th - When detachments are sent out, the commanders are to make written reports each time as to how long the troops have provisions, and the commanders are to allow no retention of the same. Pending further orders, the troops are to receive rice instead of flour two days in the week.

The colonel orders that the inspecting officer is to be present with the guard every time the parole is announced.

The 19th - The old tents are to be delivered to War Councilor Lorenz.

The 20th - Those staff officers and staff personnel who have lost horses due to enemy action are to report to the quartermaster general, who will pay for the same at fifteen schillings for each one.

The 21st - General Schmidt's Brigade will supply the following men to a chasseur company which Captain [Georg von] Hanger of the Hessian Jaeger Corps is to command, and which is to be formed from the Hessian infantry regiments at this place.

Prince Charles Regiment will provide one non-commissioned officer, one drummer, and eleven privates.

Truembach Regiment will provide one non-commissioned officer and ten privates.

Mirbach Regiment will provide one non-commissioned officer and ten privates.

Seitz Regiment will provide one non-commissioned officer, and nine privates.

Healthy and robust men are to be taken for this duty and men who are sure not to desert, therefore dependable men must be assigned. They are to be prepared to march on the shortest notice.

The colonel orders that the soldiers chosen to fill the order are to be kept separate, and assigned no duties outside of camp.

The 22nd - Nothing.

The 23rd - Those officers who are assigned to the chasseurs, are to report at the Morris house at ten o'clock in the morning on the day after tomorrow, the 25th of this month, with their weapons, etc., where

Mirbach Order Book

they will be inspected by His Excellency, General von Knyphausen. Each one assigned will have the specifications of the sizes for his uniforms and accessories with him. Pay will be advanced to the end of the month.

The 24th - The field requisitioning will be given to the chasseurs in proportion from their regiments.

The regiments are to obtain from the chasseur company that which is owed each individual for pay and allowances, and what one or another has assigned, and submit this information to Paymaster Schmllidt for disbursement.

The 25th - The colonel orders that any soldier who badgers the English, or tries to sell rum, or his uniform items, will be punished by running the gauntlet twelve times.

The 26th - Nothing.

The 27th - In the future no soldier is to cross on the Brooklyn Ferry without a pass. Officers and soldiers on duty pay nothing for the passage while on duty.

No boat shall sail after nine o'clock in the evening except in special circumstances.

The colonel orders that no baggage servant, officer servant, or anyone else, is to be entered in a report without the staff first having reviewed it.

The 28th - It is announced to the regiment that His Serene Highness, the Landgrave, is pleased to promote Ensigns Wiesemueller, von Biesenrodt, von

Mirbach Order Book

Bilsingsloewen, von Drach, and Brener to second lieutenant.

From five to seven o'clock tomorrow morning the clumsy individuals of each company will be drilled by an officer.

The 29th and 30th - Nothing.

The 31st - The commanders of the British Grenadiers and Light Infantry are to again assemble their respective battalions, as quickly as possible, at Flatbush on Long Island. The Caldonians, or North British Volunteers, previously commanded by Captain Suderland are henceforth under the command of Lord Cathcart's Legion.

August

The 1st - The picket at General Clinton's house is to be discontinued until further notice.

The 2nd - Nothing.

The 3rd - No soldier is to be allowed to go into the city on leave this evening nor tonight.

As the 35th Regiment is greatly fatigued, another English regiment from Long Island will relieve the city watch.

The 4th - The general-in-chief is very well pleased with the skill which the troops displayed in stopping the fire.

The 5th - Between ten and twelve o'clock tomorrow, Fusilier Nicolaus Schumann, sentenced to death, will be executed by the Hereditary Prince

Mirbach Order Book

Regiment at the Common Place.

The 6th, 7th, 8th, and 9th - Nothing.

The 10th - It is announced that Colonel [William] Porter will review the Stein Brigade tomorrow at eleven o'clock. Therefore, the von Mirbach Regiment will be ready for that at twelve o'clock tomorrow noon at the Place d'Armes.

The colonel orders that during tomorrow's muster everyone will appear at his very best. The officers will wear their wool shirts, white linen trousers, and white sashes.

The 11th, 12th, and 13th - Nothing.

The 14th - The colonel orders that each individual is to be told that the trees and such items as stand about the camp are not to be torn down. The first one caught will suffer the most severe punishment. As soon as it is dark, the field as well as the fire watch, is to be sent on patrol around the camp when relieved, and arrest any suspicious persons. The officers, who have something to report at parade, are to do so before the changing of the guard.

The 15th, 16th, 17th, and 18th - Nothing.

Mirbach Order Book

The 19th - Extract of the gracious letter of His Serene Highness, dated, 20 April 1778.

I hope the damage to the uniforms and some bolts of cloth, which occurred when they were being shipped to America, will be of no great consequence, and that those companies which were affected, can be helped with the raw cloth and extra uniforms, which they received at the same time. According to the accounts of the uniform commission, everything for the entire corps should have been sent from here, so that no uniforms or caps should be missing. The necessary orders have been given to the mentioned uniform commission some time ago, to fill requisitions submitted by the corps for the field regiments as quickly as possible, and I do not doubt that those orders will be carried out. The replacement of the advances made on the orders of the dead Lieutenant General von Heister to the regiments in the first campaign, as well as the restitution by them, which has been received in the previous year can not be written off by the regiments, because everyone in every war, according to the understanding and predetermined rules, have made the reparation costs set by the lieutenant general the responsibility of company chiefs. Therefore, that fund which must be applied must come from the recruiting fund, and that provided as a result of vacancies. In addition, let it be further known at guard mount that Lieutenant Colonel

Mirbach Order Book

Wittemus has been promoted to colonel with the Carabiniers, and Riding Master Klockher has been promoted to major in the Hussar Corps. It is also announced that the regiments are ordered, that just as it is commonly done in Hesse, so the officer efficiency reports are to be submitted at the end of the year, and remarks about the attention to duty and conduct and attitude toward the service of all officers are to be made without the least reservation. Not all regiments have as yet complied with this. The Grenadier Battalions must also submit these forms on subordinate officers.

It is further made known that the previous gentlemen d'armes named to the Swiss Guard have been augmented to [blank] men from Switzerland. They have seniority immediately after the Guard Regiment. Major General von Jungkenn is named commander, and Captain von Hachenberg of the 1st Battalion is designated as the lieutenant.

Also at the start of the month, a noble cadet corps was organized with Colonel Wittemus as colonel and commandant, and Professor Mauvillon as captain. It has a strength of thirty men, not counting supernumeraries, and has also been provided with the necessary non-commissioned officers, instructors, and drill masters. They are quartered in the Art Institute [Kunsthaus] which now becomes the Military Institute.

Mirbach Order Book

Dated, 21 May 1778

Concerning the Jaeger assignments of non-commissioned officers and privates, it is my intention that the same are not to be accepted until they have actually arrived in America.

[I have skipped a portion of the German text between pages 126 and 129.]

The 20th, 21st, 22nd, and 23rd - Nothing.

The 24th - All firing on the island, especially that near the general-in-chief's house, is once again strictly forbidden.

The 25th and 26th - Nothing.

The 27th - All leaving of camp by the soldiers unless accompanied by non-commissioned officers is again strictly forbidden by the colonel.

The present recruits are to be assigned to the companies of the colonel and the major. In the future however, they will be assigned equally, regardless of the losses sustained by the companies.

The 28th, 29th, and 30th - Nothing.

The 31st - Company commanders must now repeat the previously given order very minutely, that the soldiers are not to be given leave to remain outside the camp after retreat, and the tent commanders must strictly add that no man is to be allowed outside the tent after retreat. It is necessary for their benefit that this cease, and even more so that the soldiers not be allowed to drink and gamble in any suttler's tent until

Mirbach Order Book

daybreak, as has occurred on past nights, from which all sorts of disorders have arisen. The non-commissioned officers or tent commanders who fail to adhere to this order shall be locked up in the stocks for 24 hours. If a non-commissioned officer, however, participates in this drinking and gambling in a settler's tent, he shall be placed in arrest, questioned, and court-martialed. The privates will be punished by running the gauntlet twelve times, however. Primarily however, I hold the company commanders responsible for maintaining discipline and order, and they are not to allow or consent to the soldiers doing other duties, except those duties of a military nature.

C. von Romrod

The watch is to send patrols into the settlers' tents, and if soldiers are found therein after retreat, they are to be arrested.

Mirbach Order Book

September

The 1st, 2nd, 3rd, and 4th - Nothing.

The 5th - The colonel orders that during the reading of orders this evening, the companies are to be informed that the first individual who commits a crime against his comrades, or any other person, even if it be the stealing of only a needle, is to be tried immediately and sentenced by a court-martial, to running the gauntlet twelve times, and punished even more severely if warranted by circumstances.

Tomorrow morning, all recruits who have not sworn an oath on the flag, are to be ready at seven o'clock. All those who can not be present, must be notified so that they can take the oath at some other time.

The 6th - Every morning, between six and eight o'clock, the clumsy individuals and recruits are to be drilled by a company office. If the colonel sees clumsy individuals on parade in the future, the company commander will be held responsible.

All new recruits are to be drilled this evening.

The 7th, 8th, and 9th - Nothing.

The 10th - The colonel orders that in the future the password is to be given after tattoo.

Mirbach Order Book

If a 1st sergeant forgets something about the commands in the future, he is to be placed in arrest immediately and locked in the stocks.

From the 10th to the 17th - Nothing.

The 18th - Those making cartridges are to receive no additional pay in the future.

The 19th - As General Schmidt considers it fair, until the Prince Charles Regiment can again send out pickets, the Truembach and Mirbach Regiments are to serve alternately at Bunker Hill. Those regimental adjutants shall make the necessary arrangements among themselves.

The 20th, 21st, 22nd, and 23rd - Nothing.

The 24th - The Ensigns Albus and Horn, who have been in Hessen service up to this time, have been assigned to the English army with the rank of ensign, and are to have command over the non-commissioned officers and privates of the Brunswick troops who have been exchanged by, or have fled from the enemy.

The 25th - Nothing.

The 26th - General Schmidt herewith notifies the Hessian regiments that as of 1 October, the wool or leather trousers are to be worn. Also, as of 1 October, the general orders that the regiments are to drill twice a week before their quarters, from eight to ten, or at most eleven o'clock. The two days are Tuesday and Thursday. However, if the weather is bad on those

Mirbach Order Book

days, or if the regiment is on watch, they are to use another day.

The colonel orders that compliance with the above order will insure that as of 1 October the watch wear wool trousers, and that they be worn for all duty.

The 27th and 28th - Nothing.

The 29th - Tattoo is to be fired when the cannon shot is fired at eight o'clock.

Guard mount is to be held at nine o'clock in the morning.

The work detail at Bunker Hill is cancelled.

The regiment is to be prepared for drill at seven-thirty in the morning. As the recruits and convalescents for the regiments in Rhode Island are to be embarked, General Schmidt orders that those troops be sent to Captain Faetz' quarters at three-thirty, and placed under the command of Ensign Klingsoehr of the Landgrave Regiment. The length of time for which the soldiers have been provided with pay and provisions is to be given to Ensign Klingsoehr in writing.

October

The 1st and 2nd - Nothing.

The 3rd - As Admiral [John] Byron will enter the city today, he will be given a guard of one officer, one non-commissioned officer, one drummer, and 21 privates.

Mirbach Order Book

The 4th, 5th, and 6th - Nothing.

The 7th - Lieutenant [Christoph Ludwig] von Romrod will be buried at three o'clock this afternoon. The brigade officers are requested to pay their last respects and to follow the body.

From the 8th to the 19th - Nothing.

The 20th - In the future the army wagon horses are to have a full ration of hay and oats.

As drilling will cease the end of this month, General Schmidt orders that from now on the entire battalion is to drill together.

Captain Francis Lord Rawdon is named adjutant general of the army in North America, with the rank of lieutenant colonel in the army.

From the 20th to the 30th - Nothing.

The 31st - The von Truembach Regiment will bury the dead Lieutenant von Freyten of the Seitz Regiment at four o'clock tomorrow afternoon.

November

The 1st - Nothing.

The 2nd - As of tomorrow the watch in the city hall will be relieved at ten o'clock The Truembach Regiment will relieve all the security guards of the Prince Charles Regiment.

The 3rd, 4th, and 5th - Nothing.

The 6th - Captain [Henrich Wilhelm] Reuting of the Prince Charles Regiment is named city major.

Mirbach Order Book

The 7th - Nothing.

The 8th - As the von Truembach Regiment has orders to march to Kingsbridge tomorrow, today's duty assignments are changed, and the Mirbach Regiment will assume those which were ordered done by the Truembach Regiment.

If soldiers of the regiment have given money to the Scribe Stoppel for him to send to Hesse, they are to report to War Councilor Lorenz, so that it can be determined if such was delivered to the treasury, and if it was sent to Hesse.

From the 8th to the 13th - Nothing.

The 14th - The regiments are to make their various quarters, and to enter them as soon as possible without further orders. As soon as this happens, the commanders of the regiments are to make a report to the adjutant general.

The 15th - The colonel orders that prior to undertaking the planned march, the coats for the sentries be taken along.

The 16th - The craftsmen and laborers from each corps who are to be used to repair quarters and build huts, shall be paid for every day that they work between 24 October and 24 December, inclusive. The craftsmen at one schilling three pence, and the laborers at six pence sterling, for which the 25 December list will be submitted, after being signed by the commander of each corps.

Mirbach Order Book

<u>The 17th and 18th</u> - Nothing.

<u>The 19th</u> - Captain O'Reilly of the Hessian Grenadiers is named city major of New York, vice Captain Reuting.

Lieutenant Carlon of the late 112th Regiment is named assistant barracks master, and in the future all officers or other persons are to apply to him for quarters.

<u>The 20th to the 23rd</u> - Nothing.

<u>The 24th</u> - The colonel orders that everyone be prepared to march at a moments notice.

<u>The 25th</u> - Nothing.

<u>The 26th</u> - As complaints have been made to the Hessian commissariat that the regiments and battalions are drawing few, or even no uniform accessories, but obtain them at the public auctions, where spoiled items are often purchased for a small price, his excellence, the lieutenant general repeats that if the captains can not buy good items of equipment elsewhere for the soldiers, they should draw them from the commissariat.

<u>The 27th</u> - The regiment is to be ready to march at nine o'clock tomorrow. The tents are to remain standing until they are dry, then the guards are to take them down and send them to the baggage house in wagons. The quartermaster sergeant and guard are to be ready at daybreak, in order to be in quarters before the regiment.

Mirbach Order Book

<u>The 28th</u> - Nothing.
<u>The 29th</u> -   <u>Regimental Order</u>

The guards are to form at ten o'clock tomorrow morning. The staff watch is to assemble at the Colonel's; the ferry and the ships' guard, however, at Captain Rothe's quarters. The Leib Company is to send its entire guard to the staff watch. Baurmeister's Company is to provide six men at McGowan' Pass daily. Major von Wilmowsky's Company is to provide three men for the major's quarters. All the other troops ordered on guard are to assemble together at Captain Rothe's quarters. Tattoo is to be beaten at eight o'clock in the evening at the staff, as well as at the ferry watch, the same as at morning reveille. The officer from the ferry watch is to report everything that occurs at the ferry and aboard the ships to Captain Rothe, who in turn is to report any changes to the staff. During the night, some members of the watch are to remain in all the quarters at all times. Fires and lights are to be tended, to insure that no accidents result in a fire, and therefore the chimneys must be cleaned each week. Captains and company commanders are to use every consideration to prevent disorders or excesses in the quarters, and to this end a company officer is to visit each quarters everyday, and give special attention to the fires, the chimneys, and the soldiers' personal belongings, and each time

Mirbach Order Book

report this to the company commander. The latter is to inspect the quarters at least twice a week, but the days when this is to be done are left to his discretion. In case of an alert, the Leib Company is to form immediately before the flags; Major Baurmeister at Mc Gowan's Pass; and the other companies at the cannons, pending further orders, and await further orders there.

How and where the firewood is to be obtained is to be ordered later. Until then, the companies will have to fend for themselves as best as possible.

The captains and company commanders are responsible for doing everything possible to insure conservation, good order, and cleanliness in the companies. As soon as the guard in the Linsing camp, which has been commanded by Corporal Hast, as well as the one presently in the vacated camp, returns, two guard units will be formed.

On orders of the commanding general no wood is to be cut in the so-called Apthorp Grove.

The 30th - The axes and saws received by the companies are to be issued at once. The companies are responsible that the items are not misused. One officer, two non-commissioned officers, and fifty privates are to be assigned wood-cutting detail everyday, and they are to cut and stack the wood where the von Linsing and von Lengerke Grenadier Battalions are stationed, but as previously ordered, the so-called Apthorp Grove is to left alone. The wagon master is to assign wagons to pick up the wood, and to deliver it to the stack at the staff watch.

December

The 1st - Wood is not to be sent away from here under any pretext, and the commanding officer of the Hessian brigade at McGowan's Pass, is to control the use of this wood for the troops under his command, and enforce this order at McGowan's Pass and at the John's house.

The guards with General [Charles] O'Hara and at Harlem, as well as the two pickets previously detached from the von Mirbach Regiment, are to be provided by Colonel von Loose, from the regiments of his brigade.

In case of an alert, Baurmeister's Company is to march immediately to Harlem. The Leib Company and the remainder of the Colonel's Company, which are along the road, are to proceed at once to the flags, without first going to the captain's quarters. All guards and pickets are to watch for the firing of the alert rocket, which is to be fired by Fort Independence, and report this. On orders of the colonel, Quartermaster Sergeant [Johann Georg] Noll is to receive all provisions, beer, etc., and he is to be released from all other duty.

The 3rd - At precisely eight o'clock this morning

all the companies are to assemble at the colonel's quarters. The troops are to take nothing with them except their blankets, and some kettles. The Leib Company is to wait at their quarters area for the regiment. The provisions are to be received and brought along. All guards are to remain in place, and one man is to be left behind in each quarters. The pickets are to march with the regiment.

<u>Headquarters, Courtland's House,</u>
<u>3 December 1778</u>

The regiment is to be prepared to march at daybreak tomorrow, on the shortest notice. General [William] Erskine hopes that the troops will be restrained from marauding as much as possible.

The colonel orders that the plundering by the troops is strictly forbidden, except for firewood.

<u>Headquarters, Terrytown</u>
<u>4 December</u>

The regiments are to be prepared to march on the shortest notice.

The 5th - The regiments are to be prepared to march early tomorrow morning at daybreak.

<u>Regimental Orders, Harlem</u>

The 6th - The guards left behind in the quarters are to remain there until tomorrow morning. As soon as the companies at the brewery separate, they are to march to their quarters. The troops of Baurmeister's Company and the Colonel's Company, which are

Mirbach Order Book

camped on the road, are to bring the flags, under Captain Rodemann, to the colonel's quarters. If the quarters of Captain Bilsingsloewen have not been vacated, that is to take place tomorrow. At the same time, weapons are to be issued tomorrow. The officers are personally to attend to this. The ammunition is to be protected, as well as the weapons. All uniforms and uniform items and the leather items are to be cleaned as quickly as possible and placed in the best condition. The officers are to inspect these items day after tomorrow.

The 7th - Nothing.

The 8th - The colonel orders that in the future the pickets are to be at his quarters at three-thirty, so that they will be ready to move out at precisely four o'clock.

The corps' alarm posts covering the outer posts of New York Island [Manhattan] are as follows:

English Troops

The 17th Regiment before their huts, and to send a reinforcement to Fort Independence in case of an alarm.

The 44th Regiment, to form at the most advantageous place near the blockhouse on Laurel Hill.

The 57th Regiment in front of their barracks.

Hessian Troops

The Leib Regiment in front of their huts, and to

Mirbach Order Book

send a reinforcement to Spitting Devil and Prince Charles Regiment redoubts, as already ordered by Lieutenant General von Knyphausen.

The von Truembach Regiment, three companies into Fort Knyphausen, and two before Colonel von Gose's quarters.

The von Donop Regiment in front of their huts.

The Mirbach Regiment, three companies with the artillery at Harlem Ferry, and two companies to remain in the main road in front of Falkner's house.

The Lossberg Regiment in front of their cantonments, and to send a reinforcement to McGowan's Pass.

The Knyphausen Regiment is to be ordered to McGowan's line.

Provincial Troops

Royal American Regiment before their huts.

Emmerich's Chasseurs to the King's Redoubt, Thetarts and White to all the outer posts, and to patrol on the side toward which the alarm sounded, to pull back at once to this side of the defenses, and everyone to be under arms. General Tryon approves of the hand sleds, and has ordered the engineers to make two such sleds for Forts Knyphausen and Independence.

Regimental Orders

In case of an alert, the Leib Company and Major Baurmeister's Company, with the troops from the Mill, are to march at once to the beer brewery, and the latter are to allow the troops which are in a house with the Colonel's Company at Harlem, to join the Colonel's Company. On the other hand, the Lieutenant Colonel's Company and Major Wilmowsky's Company, are to remain in Harlem with the cannons. Those troops from the Colonel's Company which are on the main road, are to move at once to the flags, in order to escort them and the adjutant to Harlem, and the three companies stationed there.

In the future, the reserve picket is to consist of one officer, two non-commissioned officers, one drummer, and 25 privates.

<u>The 9th</u> - The colonel herewith notifies the company commanders that he finds it strange that the regiments are missing an unbelievable number of cartridges, as the regiments have been doing garrison duty throughout the entire summer, and it has not been necessary to load their weapons. It also seems strange how the number of missing cartridges varies so among the companies, because from the first returns of forty cartridges per man, some companies are missing 1,000 rounds, and from others thirty, and there seems no alternative but that they have been shot up while hunting. All missing rounds are to be replaced this time, and when, during inspections [in the future] one is missing without having been employed usefully, the colonel will hold the company commanders solely responsible, and they will be held

Mirbach Order Book

accountable.

On order of the colonel, the artillery horses are to be used for no purpose without his knowledge, except for hauling their own provisions, forage, and wood.

Brigade Orders

The English and German troops are to receive a proportional number of gloves for the non-commissioned officers and privates next Thursday, Friday, and Saturday, at the quartermaster general store. Those English regiments which receive gloves must do so from the regimental quartermasters, and give a receipt for the same. It is also announced that the items will be delivered without fail, and any then missing, must be paid for.

The 10th - If the weather is bad tomorrow or in the future, work details are to be cancelled.

The 11th - To prevent loss of too many cartridges, those which have damaged paper, must have the covering replaced, for which purpose each company is to obtain two books of paper, for which the company proprietor is to be charged. In the future, however, the company commanders are not to be surprised if required to pay for the paper out of their own purses. The cartridges which stick together, due to the rain should be ground into powder again, and if this powder is then worthless, it should be issued as exercise ammunition, forty rounds per man. The colonel recommends that the company commanders give special attention to the cartridges, and holds them responsible whenever cartridges are wantonly wasted. The companies are to receive exercise ammunition at Harlem next Monday. During this time, the covering material is to be prepared.

The 12th - In case of an alert, the reserve picket which is at Harlem is to assemble at the cannons. The others, however, are to remain at the company.

When the provost marshal, in carrying out his duties, requests a detachment from the regiments for his assistance, it is to be provided at once.

The 13th - If the Leib Company and Major Baurmeister's Company can make the necessary firewood near their quarters, they are to do so, and move it to the quarters in their wagons.

The Lossberg and Knyphausen Regiments are to provide a picket of one non-commissioned officer and six privates between the von Knyphausen camp and Robertson's Battalion each evening. Each regiment is to provide a captain of the day, under whose command all guards, detachments, and pickets are to be placed. The sentries of the guard and pickets must be particularly attentive when the alert signal at Fort Knyphausen sounds, and give immediate notice thereof. That signal consists, according to the order of 4 June, in three cannon shots, at one minute intervals, with two rocket firings, at two minute intervals, and fired two minutes after the last cannon shot.

Mirbach Order Book

accountable.

On order of the colonel, the artillery horses are to be used for no purpose without his knowledge, except for hauling their own provisions, forage, and wood.

Brigade Orders

The English and German troops are to receive a proportional number of gloves for the non-commissioned officers and privates next Thursday, Friday, and Saturday, at the quartermaster general store. Those English regiments which receive gloves must do so from the regimental quartermasters, and give a receipt for the same. It is also announced that the items will be delivered without fail, and any then missing, must be paid for.

The 10th - If the weather is bad tomorrow or in the future, work details are to be cancelled.

The 11th - To prevent loss of too many cartridges, those which have damaged paper, must have the covering replaced, for which purpose each company is to obtain two books of paper, for which the company proprietor is to be charged. In the future, however, the company commanders are not to be surprised if required to pay for the paper out of their own purses. The cartridges which stick together, due to the rain should be ground into powder again, and if this powder is then worthless, it should be issued as exercise ammunition, forty rounds per man. The colonel recommends that the company commanders give special attention to the cartridges, and holds them responsible whenever cartridges are wantonly wasted. The companies are to receive exercise ammunition at Harlem next Monday. During this time, the covering material is to be prepared.

The 12th - In case of an alert, the reserve picket which is at Harlem is to assemble at the cannons. The others, however, are to remain at the company.

When the provost marshal, in carrying out his duties, requests a detachment from the regiments for his assistance, it is to be provided at once.

The 13th - If the Leib Company and Major Baurmeister's Company can make the necessary firewood near their quarters, they are to do so, and move it to the quarters in their wagons.

The Lossberg and Knyphausen Regiments are to provide a picket of one non-commissioned officer and six privates between the von Knyphausen camp and Robertson's Battalion each evening. Each regiment is to provide a captain of the day, under whose command all guards, detachments, and pickets are to be placed. The sentries of the guard and pickets must be particularly attentive when the alert signal at Fort Knyphausen sounds, and give immediate notice thereof. That signal consists, according to the order of 4 June, in three cannon shots, at one minute intervals, with two rocket firings, at two minute intervals, and fired two minutes after the last cannon shot.

Mirbach Order Book

In the future, the reveille and retreat shots are to be fired from different redoubts, beginning at the one at Spitting Devil.

No sutler or seller of strong liquor is to sell on the far side of Kingsbridge, except those who have permission of Colonel Emmerich. No woman, child, or native person is to be carried across on Holland Ferry, but they must cross on pontoons, or on Spiting Devil bridge.

The 14th - As the Lossberg and Knyphausen Regiments are to furnish a picket consisting of one non-commissioned officer and nine privates between the Knyphausen Regiment and Robertson's Battalion, the Mirbach Regiment is to always provide the guard for General O'Hara pending further orders.

The colonel orders that as soon as something of consequence occurs at a guard or picket, it is to be reported immediately to the captain of the day.

The 15th - The companies are to have their pickets march so as to be at their assigned places at exactly four o'clock. The captain of the day is to set out the pickets, and give the posts exact instructions as to what they must do, inspect the posts of all the pickets and guards, one hour before daybreak, and report to the colonel by ten o'clock. Today the major with the captain of the day is to set out the picket posts, and they are not to be changed. Therefore, the captain should turn them over [to the next relief] as they stand.

Mirbach Order Book

In the event of an alert, the picket is to notify one sentry after the other, and the staff officer and captain of the day. The pickets must be inspected at the company.

The 16<u>th</u> - The colonel orders that the companies use the wood sparingly during the warm days, because it may often result, that because the weather turns bad, little that is already cut, can be transported.

No wagon is to go into the city or elsewhere unless so ordered, and when the wagons go to pick up wood, and the workers are no longer in the woods, the companies are to provide a few people for loading.

The 16th Dragoon Regiment is to be prepared to embark for their return to England.

The 17th - The colonel orders that the officer on wood detail is to report to the adjutant the number of cartloads of wood that are cut.

The 18th - The pontoon bridge is to be dismantled tomorrow.

As constant complaints are received from the inhabitants about cattle being stolen, therefore the so frequently given order is repeated, and the need to prevent this evil is to be read to the regiments every hour of the day, and at various times during the night. The colonel orders furthermore, that this order be strictly obeyed, and as Mr. Apthorp has again had an eight month old calf stolen, the officers are not only to inspect all the quarters very closely, and then report

Mirbach Order Book

to the major, but the company commanders must sharply warn the non-commissioned officers that such thefts and excesses, which can not take place without their knowledge, must cease. Further, the colonel recommends that such secret thefts be especially watched for.

<u>The 19th</u> - As the theft of cattle is becoming so common, and as a cow was stolen during the night at the regimental quarters area, the company commanders must take all precautions to prevent future thefts.

No one is to leave the quarters without permission, and therefore the person commanding the mess-kitchen areas to be especially responsible for the men. Therefore the officers in the company are to inspect all the quarters and messing areas, and check on the soldiers twice a day, morning and afternoon, and at various times. When they find that someone or another is missing, and the non-commissioned officer can not at once explain where the man is, the non-commissioned officer is to be sent to the staff watch in arrest, as without his knowledge, it is impossible for anyone to leave. As soon as it is dark, no one else is to be allowed to go out the door, even to go to the toilet, and three men of the night watch are to stay at each quarters, and a sentry is to stand at the door. The watch is to patrol frequently between the quarters, and anyone encountered outside the quarters is to be

Mirbach Order Book

arrested at once, and no one is to be allowed outside the quarters, for which the non-commissioned officer in the quarters, is to be alert.

No soldier is to slaughter without a permit from me, as otherwise the meat will be confiscated.

The company commanders are all to take the precautions that this order is strictly obeyed.

C. von Romrod

The sentries at McGowan's Pass are to inspect the covered wagons which are being loaded with wood.

<u>The 20th</u> - The companies are to drill the recruits from one to three o'clock during the good weather.

<u>The 21st</u> - The Hessian von Loos Brigade is to provide a picket, consisting of one non-commissioned officer and nine privates, behind the red house where the American Royalists were previously assigned.

All the tools and instruments which were delivered for use in the redoubt are to be kept under direct observation by the officers and non-commissioned officers, and every item lost or broken due to negligence is to be charged to their accounts. The staff officer of the day is to report the compliance with this order.

The soldiers are to receive two days' fresh provisions on this coming Wednesday.

The colonel orders that the companies take the necessary precautions to insure that good wood for

Mirbach Order Book

sleds must be arranged by the cartloads, and then made into sleds.

The 22nd - The colonel repeats the recent order that the butchers, if they have no permit from the colonel, are not to slaughter, and that which is with his permissions is not to take place until they have the appropriate permission of the major. If a regiment is inspected, which will frequently happen, and meat is found by one or another who does not have permission to slaughter, it is to be confiscated at once, and distributed among the regiments.

According to the previously given order that the companies are to be provided with sleds, the colonel recommends and orders that such be complied with at once.

The Lossberg and Knyphausen Regiments are to occupy McGowan's Pass from today on.

The 23rd and 24th - Nothing.

The 25th - The officer with the wood detachment is to report to the colonel every day.

The 26th - Nothing.

The 27th - When hay ships arrive at Harlem Ferry, the von Mirbach Regiment is to provide troops for unloading the same, and place sentries until it can be delivered to the proper destination. The colonel orders that this order be carried out.

Quartermaster Sergeant [Gottfried] Reinhard, because he reported too late as orderly to Colonel von

Loos, is to be sent in arrest to Harlem, and is to report in the future at nine o'clock.

The 28th and 29th - Nothing.

The 30th - The good appearance of the regiment is highly recommended. When the weather permits, troops reporting for guard duty are to do calisthenics a half hour before guard mount, and if it is cold, are to be drilled in marching.

The 31st - On the New Year tomorrow, the colonel wishes all officers much good fortune and recommends all his steadfast friendship. The officers need not concern themselves with congratulating the colonel. The drummers are not to beat their drums. The officers who wish to let the hautboists play, may do so, but should not pay the drummers or the hautboists, as the regimental quartermaster is to take care of all that. It goes without saying that shooting is not to be permitted, and all noise, in the quarters as well as in the streets, is to be prevented.

Mirbach Order Book

1779

[January]

The 1st - Nothing.

The 2nd - The companies needing shoe soles should submit their requests to the regimental quartermaster.

The 3rd - The money for uniform accessories to the end of 1778, after withholding for items received, can be received upon presenting an authorizing receipt.

The 4th - The colonel orders that the soldiers who have been prisoners, are to have their pay figured and receive all amounts due. Also, the companies are to pay the soldiers the uniform accessories allowances to the end of 1778, and the colonel is to receive an extract from each company, with the headings "needed", "has", "has received", "has coming", and "still owed" by the fifteenth of the month.

The 5th - Nothing.

The 6th - Commencing tomorrow, the staff officer of the day is no longer to report to Colonel von Loos, but a written report from the captain of the day, when there is nothing new, is to be submitted, except if something important occurs, the report is to be made in person to the staff officer who must notify Colonel von Loos. As almost no posts are manned during the day, an alert force is not necessary. In case of an alert, all reserve pickets covered by this order are to march at once to the place of attack and act as required.

Mirbach Order Book

Complaints come in that the pickets are burning fences, so that is strictly forbidden.

The 7<u>th</u> - Nothing.

The 8<u>th</u> -   <u>Signals</u>

In case of an attack:

1) If an enemy attacks one or more redoubts in the line beyond Kingsbridge, a cannon, or where there are none, a platoon fire by the post which is attacked, is to be fired. This signal is to be repeated by a cannon shot from Fort Knyphausen, and with a cannon shot and two rockets from the Morris house.

2) In case of an attack between Kingsbridge and McGowan's Pass, from the North River side, two cannon shots and two rockets are to be fired from Fort Knyphausen.

3) If the attack comes from Harlem Creek, a cannon and three rockets are to be fired, and both signals are to be repeated from Morris house. After each signal a dragoon is to be sent from Morris house to the headquarters.

The 9<u>th</u> and 10<u>th</u> - Nothing.

The 11<u>th</u> - General Tryon has learned with the greatest displeasure of the frequent desertions which are almost common among the troops under his command, and which in a war against mutinous subjects are those who His Majesty's service most relies upon. And, if they were English soldiers, those whose shameful plan it is to overthrow the

Mirbach Order Book

government, and the situation of the country, would be punished by execution, with the least mercy and most severely. The general pleads therefore not only that the officers exert every energy to prevent such shameful desertions, but also expects every soldier who is aware of the pending desertion of one of his comrades, will report the same to his officer. The general flatters himself that every private soldier who thinks like a true soldier, and values the honor of his corps, will have the good judgment never to desert, but quite the opposite, will try to discover all cases of desertion by others. However, if there should still be soldiers who forget their duty and honor, who slip away and escape the attention of their superiors, the general offers to pay the sentries of the outer posts a guinea for every deserter caught, and the patrols, and even the militia of West Chester, are to receive a like amount.

All pickets, when they move out of their posts, are to load their weapons.

<u>The 12th</u> - The officers in the redoubts are never to leave their posts during the time when they are on duty, and even less so, under any pretext, go visiting in the neighborhood, except to eat.

Because calf-skin knapsacks have been received among the uniform accessories from Hesse at various times, this is now made known to the regiments and corps, so that they can be issued by the commissariat against receipts, pending a determination of the price from Hesse. Also, pending further instructions, the yearly issue of uniform stockings is to be made at 160 pair per grenadier battalion, and 200 pair per regiment, against a receipt.

The colonel orders those companies which wish to be issued knapsacks to pick them up tomorrow.

The 13th - The colonel orders that the companies of the colonel and the lieutenant colonel are to settle their dispute over certain uniform accessories, and report when the settlement is arranged. [This appears to be the meaning, although it appears there are words missing in the German text.]

The 14th and 15th - Nothing.

The 16th - Pending further orders, the ration for the cavalry and wagon horses is to consist of ten pounds of hay and ten pounds of oatmeal, and ten pounds of hay and eight pounds of oatmeal for the riding horses for officers, who belong to the army.

The 17th - Nothing.

The 18th - The companies are to submit an account of the amount they have paid to the end of 1778 for uniform accessories, and what they still owe.

The 19th - As one of the picket huts was set on fire last night, which may have resulted from neglect or some other cause, General Tryon orders that one non-commissioned officer and three privates remain in each hut throughout the day. Therefore the colonel orders that this order be carried out, and the soldiers are to play each time [Obviously a copying error exists in the German text as it continues] and he also recommends that the company commanders give close attention to the conservation, and to the proper and regular feeding of the wagon horses, and that they not be used for any unnecessary purpose, as each is to be held responsible and accountable if one of these should suffer any harm.

The 20th and 21st - Nothing.

The 22nd - Only one private, instead of one non-commissioned officer and three privates, is to remain in each picket hut during the day. Two non-commissioned officers of Colonel von Gose's Brigade are to have supervision over the soldiers; one non-commissioned officer along the East River, the other along the North River.

If Colonel von Loos is in agreement, one from his brigade is to be adequate. No one, regardless of whom he might be, is to be allowed to pass or re-pass from Morrisania to Harlem without a written permission from General Tryon.

Regimental Orders

The colonel orders therefore that in each picket hut, one private is to remain. One non-commissioned officer is to have supervision over all the picket huts lying along Harlem Creek. One private is to remain in every hut along the North River, but no non-

Mirbach Order Book

commissioned officer is to be provided from the regiment for that area. The non-commissioned officer for the supervision must go from one hut to the next throughout the day, and respond to every incident.

The 23rd and 24th - Nothing.

The 25th - The regiment is notified to use wood sparingly, otherwise the local woods will not be adequate, due to the length of time it must last the regiments, and chopping down fruit or other trees, which belong to the houses, is strictly forbidden. It is therefore advisable that the regiments not permit other troops which have no right, to cut and haul wood away.

The regiments can obtain beer in the city if they send in their own barrels.

The colonel highly recommends the order about sparing wood.

The 26th - Nothing.

The 27th - Again during the past night, a cow was stolen from the host, where Captain Reichhold has his quarters. This theft was aided by the use of a sled to take it away, so it is clear that the order of 19 December, for a guard at every quarters, is not being carried out, nor is the order for a patrol to go from one quarters to the next. The colonel once again orders that the order be carried out exactly, and should any guard or patrol be found negligent in performing duty, he will be severely punished.

Mirbach Order Book

Promotions and Transfers

Major General von Truembach is promoted to Lieutenant general, and is to receive the vacant Woellwarth Grenadier Regiment as his own.

Major General von Bose is to receive the present Truembach Infantry Regiment.

Colonel von Kospoth is promoted to major general, and given command of the Landgraf Regiment.

Colonel von Keydel is transferred from the Guard Regiment to the Landgraf Regiment.

Major General von Wissenbach is promoted to lieutenant general of his own.

Colonel von Stieglitz is promoted to major general in the Leib Dragoon Regiment.

Colonel Friedrich Treusch von Buttlar is promoted to major general in the Schlotheim Regiment.

Captain Verna, now of the Guard Regiment, is promoted to major in the Wilcke Regiment with retention of his rank in a field regiment.

Colonel Bramer, now of the 2nd Battalion of the von Buenau Regiment, is named commander of the Balcke Regimeent.

Colonel von Horn of the Balcke Regiment is transferred to the Beck Regiment.

Major Wagehals, of the 2nd Battalion of the Seitz

Mirbach Order Book

Regiment, is transferred as such to the Beck Regiment.

Lieutenant Colonel Bramer is promoted to colonel in the 2nd Battalion of the von Buenau Regiment.

Lieutenant Colonel [Lubert Franz] Kurz is transferred as such to the von Huyn Regiment.

Lieutenant Colonel Koehler is promoted to colonel and made commander of the 1st Battalion of the vacant Woellwarth Regiment.

Lieutenant Colonel Koehler's previously held Grenadier Battalion is given to Major [Karl Wilhelm] Graf of the 1st Battalion of the von Seitz Regiment.

Captain Wezel is promoted to major in the garrison artillery.

Lieutenant Colonel von Schmidt, of the Schlotheim Dragoon Regiment, is returned to the 2nd Battalion of the von Buenau Garrison Regiment.

Captain [Johann Jakob] Oswald of the Wissenbach Regiment is cashiered, due to insubordinate conduct toward his commander, Lieutenant Colonel Porbeck.

Lieutenant [Louis de Foigny de] Monluisant of the Jaeger Corps is granted his requested discharge.

The 28th, 29th, and 30th - Nothing.

The 31st - (Copy) - Extract of the gracious letter of His Serene Highness

Dated 21 September 1778

[I have skipped a portion of the German manuscript between pages 185 and 186.]

Mirbach Order Book

Brigade Order

On the coming Monday, an officer from each regiment is to inspect the furniture, blankets, etc. delivered by the barracks master, and note this on the major's report, which is then to be forwarded to the commander.

Mirbach Order Book

February

From the 1st to the 6th - Nothing.

The 7th - As the day of the muster is unknown, the companies are to complete their lists by tomorrow evening, and send them to me, the adjutant.

As the new field requisitioned items from Hesse are expected, his excellency, the lieutenant general, would like to see that everything that was ordered has been paid for, and that items to be repaired are made useful, as this will provide an advantage for those who will need few or even no new items.

The 8th, 9th, and 10th - Nothing.

The 11th - Captains of companies are to settle the accounts of officers who have died since 1 February 1776, what they should have received, and what they actually received, up to the day of their death, and if the balance indicates a surplus or an indebtedness, and submit them to the colonel by the sixteenth of this month, as he must forward them to War Councilor Lorenz.

The 12th - The companies are to issue the short woolen trousers which are available as soon as possible, to the soldiers still needing them, so that they can be worn during the pending muster. They should not be issued before that time, however. Above all, the colonel recommends that everyone make the best possible appearance. General von Bose has taken over command of the Hessians in the region of

Mirbach Order Book

Kingsbridge.

The 15th - As the muster is to be held on the 23rd of this month, the colonel orders that no one be permitted to leave the quarters who can not be back at the regiment by next Saturday evening. One private is to remain in each quarters where there is no woman. All pickets are relieved, but the guard at the ferry is to remain. Everyone who can go with [the regiment] is to be present.

From the 15th to the 21st - Nothing.

The 22nd - Each regiment is to be mustered at its quarters at the time ordered. The colonel also orders that the regiment fall out at nine-thirty tomorrow morning, at that place on the road, by the quarters of Captain-at-Arms [Georg] Mueller, in the best possible condition.

The 23rd - On orders of General Tryon, no officer or private is to be given leave, and the regimental pickets are to allow no boat from here, nor any person, to pass without permission from General Tryon. Those soldiers who arrive here in boats are to be arrested at once, and sent to General Tryon.

The 24th - The orders given yesterday are to be followed exactly today also, especially that the pickets at Harlem are to be instructed to permit no soldiers with boats to pass or re-pass, pending further orders.

Every afternoon from ten to four o'clock, the recruits and clumsy individuals are to be drilled, as

Mirbach Order Book

well as the squad leaders, at that place where parades are held, with an officer present. All officers reporting for duty are to report at the parade each time. The soldiers are to wear their hair in four rolls.

<u>Evening, seven-forty-five</u>

General von Bose's Brigade is to relieve all English outposts, and those of the Gose Brigade, immediately.

The Mirbach Regiment is to provide three officer, nine non-commissioned officers, three drummers, and 140 privates for this purpose.

<u>The 25th</u> - The captain at Spitting Devil is to report what ships have passed up and down the North River to the staff officer of the day, every morning.

If the outposts have not been previously relieved, they are to be retained another four days, and pending further orders, are to be provided by General von Bose's Brigade. Every morning, when he is relieved, the staff officer of the day is to report to General Tryon.

The colonel orders that at every formation, all the officers and non-commissioned officers are to report at the appropriate time before the captains' quarters and be properly briefed.

<u>The 26th</u> - The staff officers of the day are to be relieved every 24 hours, and relieve each other in the line. They may stay at the von Gose Brigade, however, where facilities are available, and notify the

Mirbach Order Book

outposts where they are staying.

The 27th - The outpost redoubts are to be relieved tomorrow by the Hessians, except for the Leib Regiment, and remain there two days. The general's guard for General Tryon is to be alternated between the British and Hessians in the future. It will consist of one non-commissioned officer and twelve men, and serve for two days. The Hessians have the duty tomorrow. For the relief of the outposts, the von Donop and von Bose Regiments are to provide two captains, six officers, nine non-commissioned officers, three drummers, and 130 privates. To these, the von Mirbach Regiment is to provide one officer, three non-commissioned officers, one drummer, and 130 privates, who are to assemble at seven-thirty tomorrow morning at the Bose Regiment barracks.

Regimental Order

The colonel orders that the detachment assemble at his quarters at seven o'clock, and await the Leib Company at the beer brewery.

(Copy) - Extract of the gracious correspondence from the General War Commissariat, Dated Cassel, 23 September 1778

To Lieutenant General von Knyphausen,

Due to the complaints initially received about the shortage of uniforms accessories, preparations are known to have been taken to insure an adequate quantity of shirts, shoes, and shoe soles to supplement and provide the company chiefs with the desired quality and at the same price as they would have been able to obtain in their respective garrisons in Hesse, and this was done and shipped with various transports. How this was accomplished can be attested by Captain von Webern, and other officers who accompanied the transports.

According to the content of the new report from the Field War Commission, there is a shortage of the same items, on the other hand, because of the loss of many items due to the length of time and the unimaginable amount of completely spoiled items. Because of these conditions, we must be aware that future transports, which despite all care in the month of February, in case no small change in the situation occurs, are to depart from here, for those items nothing more can be shipped. At the same time, the war chest has therefore made a noticeable advance, which is only for the good of the corps, the least selfish reflection of the advantage, even more on the risk of danger, and therefore we wish to beseech the lieutenant general to be attentive to the overall needs of the regiments and corps, concerning the supply against the firmly established price, so that the situation receives the closest attention, and as far as possible, is firmly established.

If it is cheaper therefore, from among the recruits shipped out, or for the regiments among their

Mirbach Order Book

personnel, to seek out soldiers who are qualified as medics, hautboists, and provosts in sufficient numbers, the recruiting bonus of twenty Talers per man, the regiments, battalions, and corps are not able to determine. On the other hand, the pay for the same personnel, who have served so long as soldiers, up to the time of their employment, those captains in whose company they served, must make the final determination. Therefore we have allowed the lieutenant general to resolve this with the following stipulation, that the Field War Commissariat has already made a similar examination the fifteenth of the past month.

Extract of the gracious correspondence of the General War Commissariat to War Councilor Lorenz, Dated, Cassel, 10 November 1778

We find comments concerning the suggested company agreement between Lieutenant Colonel von Porbeck and the deceased Lieutenant Colonel Lange to be so similar in all aspects, that we can not grant our approval. Therefore we have taken this opportunity

[I have skipped a portion of the German manuscript between pages 197 and 210.]

The 28th of February - Lieutenant Colonel Stirling has expressed to the commanding general-in-chief his complete satisfaction with the good conduct of the troops which were on the expedition to Elizabethtown.

The commanding general-in-chief adds his appreciation to the flank companies of the guards and the 23rd and 63rd Regiments, for the satisfaction and courage with which they tolerated the fatigue of that expedition.

<u>Order, Morris house, 28 February</u>

The troops which were on the expedition are to receive an extra ration of rum today.

General Tryon takes this opportunity to express his complete satisfaction to the corps commanders, officers, and men of the troops under his command at Horseneck and Greenwich, for the bravery and courage with which they drove the enemy back through the defiles and over the precipices with a constant fire. General Tryon does not doubt that if those defiles and heights had been occupied by troops other than those which were so stimulated to fight for freedom, a good part of the troops would have been killed. General Tryon also gives his full thanks and praise for the willingness and eagerness and courage in bearing the fatigue which was caused by the long march, the bad weather, and the unimaginably difficult roads. The general flatters himself that the rapid retreat spared the lives of many good men. The general will take the opportunity today to make his honorable report about the good conduct of the troops

Mirbach Order Book

to the general-in-chief.

The von Mirbach Regiment is to provide an officer tomorrow for the baggage at New York.

Mirbach Order Book

March

The 1st - The outposts are to be relieved tomorrow morning as usual by the British and Hessians of Colonel Gose's Brigade, and each nation is to occupy its usual posts.

The staff officer of the day of General von Bose's Brigade is to resume his usual duties, as of tomorrow, but no longer to relieve in the line. As of tomorrow the pickets are to be as strong as they were previously.

The 2nd and 3rd - Nothing.

The 4th - General Tryon has notified the general-in-chief how much reason he had to be satisfied with the courage and enthusiasm of the troops who were under his command during the recent expedition. The general-in-chief expresses his thanks to the Royal Artillery Detachment, the 17th, 44th, and 57th Regiments of England, the Hessian Leib Regiment, the Loyal Americans, and Emmerich's Corps. The commanders of regiments and corps are to give strict attention that the gardens and outlying farms in their respective districts are not damaged, and those who violate these areas are to be severely punished.

Hutchinson,
Adjutant General

On orders of General von Bose, the regiments of his brigade are to be issued their weapons, and commence drilling twice each day with the recruits.

Mirbach Order Book

The 5th - A captain, two officers, two non-commissioned officers, and fifty privates of the British army are to assemble at seven o'clock tomorrow morning, on the grounds in front of the Leib Regiment, in order to escort a number of rebel prisoners who are to be exchanged for an equal number of British prisoners. The captain of the detachment will receive his marching orders at the assembly point.

The regiments and corps are to receive two gallons of beer for each man from the Fulckner's Brewery weekly as follows:

The 17th and 44th Regiments, the Leib and von Bose Regiments, on Mondays and Thursdays.

The Loyal Americans, Chasseurs, and von Lossberg and von Knyphausen Regiments, on Tuesdays and Fridays.

The 57th Regiment, the Artillery, and the von Donop and von Mirbach Regiments, on Wednesdays and Saturdays.

N.B. - The Hessian Artillery is included with the regiments.

The 6th - The Hessians are to provide a detachment of one captain, one officer, six non-commissioned officers, and fifty privates who are to assemble tomorrow morning, at which time the captain will receive further orders.

For this detail the von Bose Regiment is to

provide one captain, three non-commissioned officers, and 25 privates; the von Gose Regiment one officer, three non-commissioned officers, and 25 privates, for a total of one captain, one officer, six non-commissioned officers, and fifty privates.

The Lossberg Regiment is to provide one non-commissioned officer and eight privates; the Knyphausen Regiment one non-commissioned officer and nine privates; and the Mirbach Regiment one captain, one non-commissioned officer, and eight privates, for a total of one captain, three non-commissioned officers, and 25 privates.

Those in the detachment are to take provisions for only one day, but no blankets.

Regimental Orders

The detachment is to assemble at the brewery at precisely five o'clock.

The 7th and 8th - Nothing.

The 9th - The colonel orders that by 15 April, all recruits be in a condition to be assimilated into the companies and the battalions, otherwise they are to be the responsibility of the various company commanders.

The companies of the colonel and lieutenant colonel are to submit the appropriate documents to the regimental quartermaster at once.

The 10th - Nothing.

The 11th - As General von Bose has learned that

the non-commissioned officers and privates of the regiments go hunting so often as to neglect duty, he wishes the commanders of the regiments to insure that the forbidden shooting cease.

The colonel orders that those so engaged in hunting be given exemplary punishment.

The 13th - A detachment consisting of one captain, two officers, two non-commissioned officers, two drummers, and 100 privates of the British, and a like number of Hessians, are to assemble tomorrow morning at six o'clock near the cantonment of Emmerich's Chasseurs, to escort forage wagons commanded by Lieutenant Colonel Emmerich. The Emmerich Corps is to be ready at the same time. The detachment is to take along one day's rations.

The Bose Regiment is to provide one captain, one officer, one non-commissioned officer, one drummer, and fifty privates; the Gose Regiment one officer, one non-commissioned officer, one drummer, and fifty privates, for a total of one captain, two officers, two non-commissioned officers, two drummers, and 100 privates.

And the Lossberg Regiment will provide one officer, one non-commissioned officer, and sixteen privates; the Knyphalusen Regiment seventeen privates; and the Mirbach Regiment one captain, one drummer, and seventeen privates for a total of one captain, one officer, one non-commissioned officer,

Mirbach Order Book

one drummer, and fifty privates.

By ten o'clock on Monday morning, Captains Reichhold and Rodemann are to have inspected the sabers and bayonet scabbards of the Colonel's and Lieutenant Colonel's Companies.

After Orders

The ordered inspection of the saber scabbards is not to be done by Monday, but another day will be set.

The 14th - The detachment which escorted the forage wagons is to receive an extra portion of rum.

The 15th - After the regiments, battalions, and corps, except those in Rhode Island and Halifax, have settled accounts with the commissariat for 1776 and 1777, the regimental quartermaster should have no further charges to add or subtract for the yearly accounting for the companies, and the remaining staff individuals. The commanders are strictly informed to hold the regimental quartermasters thereto without any reconsiderations, that this accounting be completely finished before the start of the next campaign, especially, however, the companies and other yearly comparisons for those two years for the deceased or otherwise departed officers, be sent to the commissariat as soon as possible for revisions and certification.

New York, 13 March 1779

The 16th, 17th, and 18th - Nothing.

Mirbach Order Book

<u>The 19th</u> - As General Tryon has learned with great displeasure that the regiments on the island are firing frequently, and even with ball ammunition, General von Bose repeats once again the previously issued order that such firing is forbidden, and the perpetrators are to be severely punished. Therefore the colonel orders that on payday, on the 21st, this order is to be made known to the companies, so that no one can make the excuse that he was not aware of it, and those who continue to do so, and are caught, will be punished by running the gauntlet twelve times.

<u>The 20th, 21st, and 22nd</u> - Nothing.

<u>The 23rd</u> - Each regiment is to submit a list tomorrow morning, as to how much straw is needed for straw mattresses in the tents.

<u>The 24th, 25th, and 26th</u> - Nothing.

<u>The 27th</u> - As General Tryon is aware that some relief detachments are marching in a very disorderly manner, he orders that all watches, in the future, whether going or coming off duty, are to march in good order, and that the soldiers are thereby prevented from running around.

<u>The 28th</u> - As the colonel has learned that the pickets are not conducting themselves properly when going on watch, that they are not only to assemble before the quarters, but are to be inspected, and the non-commissioned officer is not to march them away until he has all of them in a body. If this order is

Mirbach Order Book

disobeyed, the colonel will hold the company commanders responsible.

The 29th and 30th - Nothing.

The 31st - Pay formation is to be held tomorrow morning at nine o'clock at the captains' quarters, at which time the soldiers are to be present with their cartridge pouches. They are to be inspected to ensure that they have all their cartridges.

Mirbach Order Book

April

The 1st and 2nd - Nothing.

The 3rd - The soldiers are to clean and polish all their belongings, and conduct themselves soberly over the holiday.

Letter from His Excellency, Lieutenant General Von Knyphausen to Colonel von Romrod
New York, 31 March 1779

The general pardon for deserters from my command of the graciously entrusted auxiliary corps of Hessian troops, which follows in writing, is to be observed and govern such cases as arise at the von Mirbach Regiment. The returned deserters are to be read the Articles of War once again, and administered the oath pledging the regiments to the King of England's service.

General Pardon

Of His Serene Highness, the ruling Landgrave of Hesse's Commanding Lieutenant General and Commander-in-Chief of the Auxiliary Corps of Hessian troops in the service of the King of England, Chief of a Fusilier Regiment, and Knight of the Princely Hessian Order.

I, Wilhelm von Knyphausen, make known to each and every one to whom it applies: Following His Excellency, the King of England's General-in-Chief, Sir Henry Clinton's, R.B., general pardon issued for

Mirbach Order Book

all and every deserter from the royal army on 23 February of this year who return to duty with the royal troops of their own accord, by the first of the next coming month, and which I then

[I have skipped a portion of the German manuscript between pages 125 and 127.]

Knyphausen
On order of His Excellence
Justin Heinrich Motz
Senior Auditor

- - - - - - -

The 4<u>th</u> and 5<u>th</u> - Nothing.

The 6<u>th</u> - The recruiting money can be obtained from the Field War Commissariat upon presentation of an authorizing receipt on the seventh of this month, and on the following day.

DuPuy

On orders of General Tryon, those sentries on picket duty on the North and on the East Rivers this evening, are to allow all boats passing up as well as down river, and the staff officer of the day is to report tomorrow morning, but not to mention any examination, but to allow all boats passing to pass unhindered.

The 7<u>th</u> - The order given yesterday about the boats

Mirbach Order Book

ends, and the boats as previously happened, are again to be challenged and examined.

Memorandum

His Excellency, General Clinton, will be coming out of the city sometime early tomorrow morning to inspect the fortifications and outposts. As it is not known if his excellence will take this opportunity to inspect the troops, General von Bose orders all the regiments remain available, and no one is to be granted leave from their cantonments. The regiments will be advised if they are to hold a formation.

The colonel orders that in accordance with previous orders, no one is to be granted leave, and that the officers at tomorrow's formations appear in similar uniforms. The non-commissioned officers and privates, however, are to wait in their quarters so that they can fall out at once, and make the best possible appearance.

After Orders, at Nine O'clock in the Evening

No boats passing up and down the North River during the night are to be challenged, but allowed to pass quietly and unhindered.

(Copy) Letter from Major DuPuy to
General DuPuy
New York, 7 April 1779

[I have skipped a portion of the German

Mirbach Order Book

manuscript at page 230.]

On orders of His Excellency, Lieutenant General von Knyphausen, the regiments are to commence drilling by companies from tomorrow on, at eight o'clock.

The 8th - Nothing.

The 9th - The order concerning passing boats ends again.

A detachment of one officer, three non-commissioned officers, and eighteen privates for the guard ship, which lies in the North River near Spitting Devil, is to assemble before the 17th Regiment, and march from there to the shore, where they will find a boat to take them across. This detachment will be provided by the British pending further orders, and is to be relieved every week.

The 10th - Nothing.

The 11th - The Brunswick soldiers who are here without officers, until they can be returned to their own regiments, are to do duty with the Hussars, commanded by Captain Diemar of the 60th Regiment. The following officers are assigned to the above corps, which is commanded by Captain Ferguson: Lieutenant von Molitor, previously of the Ansbach service, and Cornet Albus, previously of the Hessian service.

The 12th - Nothing.

The 13th - As Captain O'Riley has requested of the general-in-chief to be allowed to return to duty with his company, his excellence has granted that request, and designated Captain Haiveston of the 26th Regiment in his stead, as Place Major in New York.

The 14th - As the work on Laurel Hill is not considered field work, every man who works there is to receive six pence sterling per day.

The 15th - (Copy) Letter from His Excellency,
Lieutenant General von Knyphausen
to General von Bose,
Dated New York, 9 April 1779

[I have skipped part of the German manuscript, between pages 233 and 235.]

The 16th - Nothing.

The 17th - All rebel deserters, as soon as they enter the lines, are to be sent to headquarters at the Morris house.

The 18th - The guards, who are in the picket huts all day, are to return to their regiments, but the regiments are to be responsible for the huts.

The colonel orders that the guards that are in the huts during the daytime, are not to leave them, pending further orders.

The 19th - Lieutenant Sproule, engineer assistant, who has charge of the work on Laurel Hill, is to issue receipts for the number of soldiers from each regiment who are working each day, so that they can collect the money according to the recent order.

The 20th and 21st - Nothing.

Mirbach Order Book

<u>The 22nd</u> - On order of His Excellency, Lieutenant General von Knyphalusen, the Articles of War are to be read to the troops during the present training.

The furniture money is to be paid to the troops without the least deduction.

<u>The 26th</u> - Nothing.

<u>The 27th</u> -All work details are to take their weapons with them.

Extract of the gracious letter of His Serene Highness
Dated Weissenstein, 19 November 1778

The invalids of the corps in America must await approval from England, which can not take much longer. Therefore, I grant the lieutenant general full power, if and when he thinks it proper, to send the invalids home, and I fully approve that Lieutenant [Friedrich Theodor] Spencer, of the present von Bose Regiment, be sent with the same transport, under close arrest.

Dated 19 November 1778

[I have skipped a part of the German manuscript between pages 237 and 241.]

All regiments are directed to attach a rider at the end of their rank list, where the free corporals are noted, as to their conduct, so that when a vacancy exists, it can be determined here, who is or is not qualified for promotion.

Mirbach Order Book

Promotions and Transfers

Major Halzfeld is promoted to lieutenant colonel in the 2nd Battalion of the Truembach Regiment.

Major Hillebrand is promoted to lieutenant colonel in the von Huyn Regiment.

Major Graf is promoted to lieutenant colonel in the von Seitz Regiment.

Lieutenant Colonel von Kitzel of the Wissenbach Regiment, is transferred as commander of the von Seitz Regiment.

Captain [Johann Otto] Goebel of the 1st Battalion of the Truembach Regiment is promoted to major in the Wissenbach Regiment.

Captain [August Ludwig] von Hedemann of the Wissenbach Regiment and lately of the Buelow Regiment, is promoted to major in the Balcke Regiment.

Major Pauli of the Artillery Corps is graciously released from his duty.

The 28th - Nothing.

The 29th - The general pardon for all the deserters from the Hessian troops in America is extended to the end of the coming month of June, by Lieutenant General von Knyphausen.

The 30th - The regiments are to submit a signed, written extract of what the artillery officers have as credits or debts.

Mirbach Order Book

May

The 1ˢᵗ - Nothing.

The 2ⁿᵈ - The general-in-chief herewith informs the provincial troops that His Majesty the King, for their brave conduct on several occasions, has graciously resolved:

All officers of the provincial corps, who are commissioned and are to be commissioned, receive rank junior to all similar British officers. If a provincial corps officer is wounded by the enemy and loses a limb, he will receive the same prerogatives as a British officer.

The 3ʳᵈ - The following British promotions are announced:

To major general as of 19 February 1779 - Colonel Edward Mathew, Fanies Schmidt, August Prevost, James Pattison, Alexander Leslie, Sir William Erskine, and John Campbell.

To colonel as of 19 February 1779:
Lieutenant Colonels Sir Henry Calder, Arthur Martier, Wanton Poavel.

The 4ᵗʰ and 5ᵗʰ - Nothing.

The 6ᵗʰ - Regimental Orders

The colonel orders that the regiment be ready for drill at precisely eight o'clock tomorrow morning. The officers are to be uniformly clad, and the regiment is to march with its front to the brewery.

Memorandum - Possibly His Excellency,

Mirbach Order Book

Lieutenant General von Knyphausen, will observe the drill.

The 7th and 8th - Nothing.

The 9th - (Extract copy and gracious correspondence from the Hessian War Commissariat to the War Councilor Lorenz, Dated Cassel, 17August 1778)

[I have skipped a part of the German manuscript between pages 246 to 248]

Both Major Generals Stirn and Schmidt have received permission from His Serene Highness, the Landgrave of Hesse, to return to Hesse.

The 10th and 11th - Nothing.

The 12th - [Lists of the] missing artillery and royal wagon horses are to be turned in to Colonel von Cochenhausen. At the same time, the shortage of ball ammunition is to be reported, based on sixty rounds per man.

The Lossberg and Knyphausen Regiments are to move into camp outside the city tomorrow.

The 13th - Because of the bad weather, the Lossberg and Knyphausen Regiments have not marched, and will continue to do duty as before.

The 14th - Nothing.

The 15th - The Lossberg and Knyphausen Regiments are to move into camp near the city.

Mirbach Order Book

<u>The 16th</u> - Nothing.

<u>The 17th</u> - The colonel orders the companies to make pay adjustments with the soldiers to the end of 1778, and pay those having credits tomorrow. No troops are to remain in the picket huts during the daytime.

The lists for 200 days' forage money are to be submitted to the quartermaster general on 1 June.

<u>The 18th</u> - The two Hessian grenadier battalions are to provide the pickets and guards, which have been provided by the Lossberg and Knyphausen Regiments. On orders of His Excellency, Lieutenant General von Knyphausen, the companies are to settle pay accounts with their soldiers, and each man is to be supplied with a paybook. The extract is to be submitted to General von Bose, who will then ask the troops if they are satisfied with the accounting.

<u>The 19th</u> - The pickets in huts number two and three on the East River are not to be provided by the von Mirbach Regiment in the future, but occupied by the quartermaster general department.

The uniform accessories' accounts are to be explained to the soldiers, and an extract submitted to his excellency, the lieutenant general, by each company.

<u>The 20th</u> - The colonel orders that if the explanation of the uniform accessories' accounts have not been given to the soldiers in accordance with the

Mirbach Order Book

orders of the seventeenth, it is to be done with the men individually today, so that by the questioning there can be no grounds for dispute. The companies should prepare an extract covering the uniform accessories with column headings

<u>Should have</u> <u>Have received</u> <u>Have in excess</u>
Reichsthaler/Albus/Heller Rt/Alb/H Rt/Alb/Heller
and submit it to the colonel in duplicate, by Saturday evening.

As the shortage of artillery and royal wagon horses for each regiment has been made up, it is again recommended that strict attention be given, so that they are not employed for any purpose but royal service, as there is no longer a situation whereby replacements can be procured for those lost.

New York, 17 May 1779
F.C. DuPuy

<u>The 21st</u> - The uniform accessory extracts are to be signed by the company commanders as usual.

The 17th Dragoon Regiment, Light Infantry, British and Hessian Grenadiers, the 17th Regiment of Foot, Jaegers, Queen's Rangers, Loyal Americans, Emmerich's Corps, Legion, and Captain Ferguson's Detachment are to be prepared to march on the shortest notice.

<u>The 22nd</u> - The entire regiment is to assemble at four o'clock this afternoon at Harlem, to evaluate the uniform accessories' accounts. The regimental

Mirbach Order Book

quartermaster is to be present.

The 23rd - Nothing.

[The 24th] - The general-in-chief has ordered that all the firewood in the forests at Morrisania is to be kept for the troops in the Kingsbridge district. Therefore General Tryon orders that no wood is to be cut and hauled away from Morrisania after 1 June, whether it belongs to the public department or anyone else.

The 25th - The general-in-chief has informed General Tryon that His Excellence, Lieutenant General von Knyphausen, is to assume command of the Kingsbridge district, and therefore all reports are to be sent to General Knyphausen.

The 26th - The work detachment is to work from five to eleven o'clock in the morning, and from three o'clock until sunset in the afternoon.

During drill tomorrow, on orders of the colonel, the men are to have their uniform accessories' book with them.

At the end of each month, the officers are to inspect the ball ammunition and report concerning this to the major during formation. The company commanders are to give strict attention that the cartridges are protected, and not unnecessarily expended.

The Minnigerode Grenadier Battalion is to march to join the two other grenadier battalions at Marston's

Mirbach Order Book

Wharf tomorrow. The Hereditary Prince Regiment is to march to the city, and assume garrison duty. The Queen's Rangers and the British and Hessian Jaegers are to march to the William's Bridge, on this side of the Bronx. When the regiments march, they should leave a good non-commissioned officer and a few convalescents behind in the huts, to watch over their preservation.

<u>The 27th</u> - Every 24 hours the von Mirbach Regiment is to provide one non-commissioned officer and twelve men to protect the wood-cutters at Morrisania.

The work details which are working on this side of Kingsbridge are to march there commencing tomorrow, without weapons or cartridge boxes, and it is permitted for the regiments which are near their camps, to spend the noon hour therein.

<u>The 28th</u> - General von Bose as of this time, has the Leib, von Donop, and von Mirbach Regiments in his brigade.

<u>Headquarters, New York, 29 May 1779</u>

The following corps are to march into camp tomorrow, and must march out of their cantonments, so as to pass Kingsbridge by seven o'clock:

<u>The Left Column</u> - Hessian Jaegers, three Hessian grenadier battalions, and the von Bose Regiment are to march to Philipp's house.

<u>The Right Column</u> - Queen's Rangers, the 7th

Regiment, 63rd Regiment, and Legion are to march over the Bronx on the William's Bridge.

<u>The Left Central Column</u> - Ferguson's Corps, Light Infantry, 17th Dragoon Regiment, and Loyal Americans are to march to Valentine's Hill.

<u>The Right Central Column</u> - Emmerich's Corps, the 17th, 23rd, 33rd, and 64th Regiments are to march to Valentine's Hill.

Major General Vaughan commands the British, Major General Sir William Erskine commands the Cavalry and the Light troops. The six British regiments are to form in two brigades.

<u>1st Brigade</u> - The 7th, 63rd, and 17th Regiments are to be commanded by Lieutenant Colonel [Allured] Clarke, pending further orders.

<u>2nd Brigade</u> - The 23rd, 64th, and 33rd Regiments are to be commanded by Lieutenant Colonel Webster pending further orders.

It is recommended to the regimental commanders that they take no unnecessary women or children along. The wives and children left behind should be quartered in the empty tents or barracks. Therefore a list of the number of wives and children must be turned into Lieutenant Colonel Kemple, the deputy adjutant general.

Regimental Orders

<u>The 29th</u> - The regiment is to assemble this evening at six o'clock at the colonel's quarters, and enter the

Mirbach Order Book

camp where the Lossberg and Knyphausen Regiments have been. The regimental quartermaster and quartermaster sergeants are to assemble at the colonel's quarters at two o'clock. All company commanders are to report also to the colonel at two o'clock. The guards in the huts are to be discontinued.

The 30th - The grenadiers who have occupied the huts to this time are to be informed, on orders of Lieutenant General von Knyphausen, that they are not to rejoin their battalions, but are to occupy the huts not occupied by the von Mirbach Regiment.

The 31st - The guards at General von Bose, on orders of the colonel, are to gather every morning at seven o'clock at the colonel's quarters.

The picket at the Negro huts, consisting of one non-commissioned officer and twelve men, is to report this evening to 1st Sergeant Bachmann.

[I have skipped part of the German manuscript as page 260 is missing, and a question mark at the top of page 261 apparently signifies an error in copying from the original.]

Each company is to send a wagon-load of wood to the bakery.

Mirbach Order Book

June

The 1st - Companies are to send the barracks items into the city tomorrow, and bring the tents out with them for which purpose, at precisely six o'clock tomorrow morning, the wagons are to gather at Captain Rothe's hut. The wagon-master is going into the city. The day after tomorrow, the tents are to be set up in the camp, fifteen per company.

The superfluous baggage can be sent to the baggage house by the companies on the days when the wagons departing the regiment are empty.

The day after tomorrow the companies are to allow the recruits to fire the last ten rounds.

The 2nd - As the companies of the colonel, Major von Wilmowsky, and Major Baurmeister provide the baker and the bakery, the Leib Company and the Lieutenant Colonel's Company are to provide handymen who have a little knowledge of baking.

Duty Details, 2 June 1779
Watches and Pickets

The two companies at Marsten's Wharf are to provide daily:

    1) Camp guard of one non-commissioned officer, one drummer, and nine privates.

    2) At the magazine at Marsten's Wharf, one non-commissioned officer and six privates.

    3) At McGowan's Pass, one non-com-

Mirbach Order Book

missioner officer and three privates

4) A ready force of one officer, two non-commissioned officer, one drummer, and eighteen privates.

5) Instant response detachment guard at the house of the general-in-chief and a general's guard of thirty privates daily, also each company is to provide six privates one day, and on the second day include a non-commissioned officer in each of these, or twelve privates. [There is a question mark at the start of this entry, indicating a possible copying error, as it does not make complete sense.] [Total] one officer, five non-commissioned officers, two drummers, and 48 privates.

The two companies on the North River:

1) Camp guard of one non-commissioned officer, one drummer, and six privates.

2) A mobile picket of one officer, four non-commissioned officers, one drummer, and 36 privates.

3) Instant response detachment at General Clinton's house, six privates. [Total] three non-commissioned officers, one drummer, and 27 privates.

Also daily from the artillery battalion for the instant response detachment, the general guard, and General Clinton's house, five non-commissioned officers.

Mirbach Order Book

Making as total of two officers, eighteen non-commissioned officers, five drummers, and 129 privates.

<u>Memorandum</u> - The instant response detachment, the guards at General Clinton's house, the general guard, and all extraordinary duty is to be carried out by the entire regiment. The remaining ordinary duties are to be attended to by the companies themselves.

<u>The 3rd of June</u> - As complaints have been received that the farmers who bring cattle here are being stopped by the troops and forced to sell them at a certain price, Lieutenant General von Knyphausen orders that practice to cease. The people with their cattle are to pass unhindered, and the chief provost has been ordered to give this matter his attention.

<u>Regimental Orders</u>

The officers are herewith advised to send their unnecessary and surplus equipment to the baggage house, because otherwise they will risk having overloaded wagons if ordered to march. The equipment would then need to be unloaded and nothing would be available which would be needed by the company. Various orders have been given previously that the wagons not be overloaded nor used unnecessarily. Even if they are moving rather empty, the non-commissioned officers and privates are not to ride nor are they to be driven at a gallop. This is sharply forbidden, and as the regiment presently is so

Mirbach Order Book

widely scattered that the wagons can not be driven to the fire guard, but must be kept at the companies, the colonel charges the company commanders to take all necessary precautions to conserve the wagons and horses.

The 4th - Tomorrow morning at seven o'clock the companies are to be in their camps ready for drill. The companies are to be divided into four platoons, and the commanders in the camps may permit the firing of cartridges according to their own discretion. The troops are to leave the ball cartridges behind protected in their knapsacks.

The 5th - The two companies at Marston's Wharf as well as those at John's house are to be divided from the troops detached from the Leib Company, but are to be responsible for their messing, and are to receive rations for them. At every second issue of bread the remaining flour is to be issued and therefore the companies must be supplied with bags.

The 6th - Nothing.

The 7th - On orders of His Excellency, Lieutenant General von Knyphausen, the drill, during which the regiments fire cartridges, is to cease.

The 8th, 9th, and 10th - Nothing.

The 11th - The soldiers on pass, who wish to pass the outposts, are not to be allowed to cross the Kingsbridge, but must go over the Deickman Bridge, where they are to show their pass to the commanding

Mirbach Order Book

officer, and be allowed to cross. The officers, non-commissioned officers, and privates on duty however, may cross over the Kingsbridge.

The 12th - Next Monday a packet boat is to sail to Europe.

The 13th to 22nd - Nothing.

Headquarters, Philippsburg, 22 June 1779

Commencing now and pending further orders, the troops are to receive the following portion of oats:

For the riding horses of the generals, staff officers, and other officers attached to the staff and actually serving in the field, eight pounds of oats daily.

For the cavalry, eight pounds daily.

For the wagon horses on the march, six pounds daily.

But when not on the march they are to receive only four pounds daily.

The horses of the adjutants and regimental quartermasters receive their same portions as the wagon horses. The other officers of the infantry, not included herein, are to receive absolutely no oats pending further orders.

DuPuy

The 23rd and 24th - Nothing.

The 25th - As the colonel has received complaints that the soldiers enter the gardens of residents even on the streets in this neighborhood, and take vegetables

Mirbach Order Book

and even unripe potatoes, it is ordered that during payday tomorrow, the often given order against stealing from gardens is to be repeated to each man, and made clear that this order is to be strictly observed. Anyone who violates it, without further investigation or consideration, is to run a gauntlet of 200 men twelve times. To this end, the commanders in the company camps are to read it at various times during the day, as well as at night, so that the companies can not claim that any man, except those at church services, has not been present during a reading, and therefore can not be excused. Therefore the troops who are absent when this order is read tomorrow, and those who are absent on another day, when they are present, will have had the order read to them.

Everyone who receives rations and bread, except the women and children, is to have one pence withheld at pay formation tomorrow. The regimental quartermaster is to personally withhold this from the companies, and pay it to the bakers.

The 26th to 30th - Nothing.

Mirbach Order Book

July

The 1st and 2nd of July - Nothing.

The 3rd - On orders of His Excellency, Lieutenant General Clinton, Colonel von Hachenberg is to perform duty as a brigadier.

The 4th - Only one regimental quartermaster per brigade, and the necessary escort, is to be sent to receive the pay and allowances from the Field War Commissariat for all the scattered regiments and corps. Each is to be provided with the proper authorization papers and other receipts from the regiments and deliver them for whatever they are to receive.

The 5th - Nothing.

The 6th - Major General Paterson is named commandant at New York pending further orders.

The army is hereby notified that Major Bruen, deputy quartermaster general, is prepared to pay forage money for 200 days against lists submitted after 1 June.

The 7th, 8th, and 9th - Nothing.

Headquarters, Marmaroneck, 10 July 1779

As the general-in-chief has had complaints from the residents that their forage has been maliciously destroyed by the soldiers, his excellence orders that when a detachment from the army marches, it is to be accompanied by a commissary, who is to buy hay, or

Mirbach Order Book

indicate where each corps can graze, and the owners -- if loyal to the King -- are each to receive receipts so that everything which they supply to the army can be paid for. His excellence furthermore, expects that the commanding officers of corps will take the necessary steps to ensure that their troops take nothing from the inhabitants except that which has been authorized for them.

Whenever the army enters a new camp, the regimental quartermaster and heads of various departments are to camp near the commissary, on the right wing of the line, and await instructions there.

Hutchinson
Deputy Adjutant General

At nine o'clock tomorrow morning the 200 day advance forage money from 1779 is to be paid out by the regimental quartermasters against receipts.

From the 11th to the 15th - Nothing.

The 16th - On orders of Lieutenant General von Knyphausen the pickets along the North River are to carry weapons. The colonel orders that this order be strictly obeyed, and close attention is to be paid that the cartridges are not wasted in an unnecessary manner.

From the 17th to the 20th - Nothing.

The 21st - Commencing today, the Leib Regiment is to provide three privates for the picket on the North River, and they are to provide a post at a burned out

Mirbach Order Book

spot in the woods to the right of the picket, and establish communication with the Donop Regiment pickets to their right. On the other hand, they are to cancel the picket near the tents at Harlem, but during the night a soldier is to sleep in the tents on the right and left flanks, in order to give some security to the camp. Further, the colonel orders that all the pickets are to make frequent patrols.

The 22nd - When the next pay and allowance monies are received, half of the uniform and accessories money can also be received.

The 23rd, 24th, and 25th - Nothing.

The 26th - The Landgraf Regiment which marched here this morning and occupied the area which the 17th Regiment had occupied, is assigned to the brigade of General von Bose. However, pending further orders, it is free of all duty.

The 27th - The order that no one is to dare to cut the grass in the meadow, nor to take hay away, is repeated once again, and his excellence will severely punish anyone who goes against this order.

The guard at Kingsbridge, according to orders is to allow no one to cross Kingsbridge without a pass, nor is he to allow soldiers or servants to carry hay across.

As the care of the sick can not be administered as well in the unhealthy huts as in the hospital, the colonel orders the companies to send their sick individuals to the hospital.

Mirbach Order Book

<u>The 28th</u> - As the Hessian Grenadiers are to occupy the John house on the North River, the companies are to march away from there at six o'clock tomorrow morning and occupy the camp by the companies at Marston's Wharf.

<u>The 29th</u> - The von Mirbach Regiment is to provide the pickets on the North River, as previously, pending further orders.

As, according to the above order, the duty can not yet be altered, and is to be provided on the East River by the four companies commencing today, the colonel orders the four companies to also provide the pickets jointly on the North River.

The officers at Harlem are to make no inspection on the East River, but an officer is to conduct an inspection at Harlem daily. The pickets moving out to go on duty are to be inspected at the same time by the above officer. First sergeant [Johann Jacob] Weissenborn is to have command over the non-commissioned officers and privates of the four companies on ordinary duty, and carry out the orders as he has done in the past.

<u>The 30th</u> - As Major DuPuy has sought permission from His Serene Highness to serve in the regiment and to be released from his previous duty of brigade major, which has graciously been granted, Captain [Friedrich Wilhelm] Werner, of the Artillery Corps, has been named henceforth as the brigade major.

Mirbach Order Book

The following gracious orders of His Serene Highness are herewith made known to the regiments, battalions, and corps:

Second Lieutenant [Karl Josef] Juliat, of the Landgraf Regiment, has been released.

Second Lieutenant [Werner] von Ferry, of the Knyphausen Regiment, has been granted his release, which he had requested of the Chancery in Hesse.

As Captain [Friedrich] von Malsburg of the Ditfurth Regiment, who for some time has commanded men of the Regiment, has distinguished himself at the affair at Rhode Island, on 29 August of last year, according to all reports received by His Serene Highness, that ruler has conferred the Orden pour la vertu Militaire on him.

Werner

<u>The 31st</u> - From now on, there is to be a staff officer of the day, who is to send a written report to his excellence when nothing of consequence occurs.

The outposts are to be relieved tomorrow morning, and at six o'clock, and according to the plan, be occupied before the army moves out, ahead of the line. The British are to occupy Forts Independence, Number 8, and Number 5, with the following regiments: 7th, 23rd, 44th, and 57th. The following Hessian regiments are to relieve the outposts: Leib, Landgraf, Prince Charles, Donop, and von Bose.

The regiments and battalions on the North River

Mirbach Order Book

are to establish their outposts as appropriate so as to form an orderly chain.

Extract Report from the War Commissariat General, dated 19 April 1779

[I have skipped part of the German manuscript between pages 280 and 281.]

Extract Report from the War Commissariat General dated 19 April 1779

(The charge for the forage received in nature is nothing new, consequently, it causes us no little astonishment, that the officers consider themselves entitled to express any dissatisfaction. Should it be a positive fact, that the officers belong to the honorable corps are to have this at any rate necessary forage that is delivered to them in nature, as a gift, and gratis in the same way as the officers of the English army, the charge made for this will cease of itself, and the amount which has been retained for this purpose, and which is merely nominal and very small, will always be of use to everybody. Should the reverse be the case, however, the natural agreement with regard to the fixed charges, which has never been disputed, will be carried out.)

(Extracted on 31 July 1779)

Extract of correspondence dated 22 February 1779

Mirbach Order Book

(And should an officer not always be able to do duty, the desired return to Hesse must not be made easy for him straightway, but a very careful examination must be made first of all, as to whether the given reasons are well-founded, and whether he really is not able to take part in future campaigns any longer. Upon the whole, I hereby repeat the commands which I have issued at different times concerning this matter, namely, not to grant any officer leave without first enquiring of me and receiving permission to do so, and even when permission has been given by me, not to allow any one to return here by any other opportunity except by a transport with invalids, in order to save the very considerable expense, except of course, something particular should have occurred, for which special orders are to be issued, &c. &c. It is also to be enjoined on all the regiments and battalions of the corps in America, that the regimental quartermaster is to keep a detailed diary of every single event which concerns the battalion or regiment from the commencement of the journey to America, in order that same can be delivered to me on the return of the regiment, and be preserved by same.)

Extract of Correspondence, dated 1 April 1799
The following officers departed from here on the past Monday, under the command of Colonel von Keydel, and are assigned to the corps in America.

Mirbach Order Book

Captain [Karl Ludwig] Doernberg of the infantry is to do duty with the von Linsing Grenadier Battalion.

First Lieutenant [Johann Ernst] von Witzingerode to serve with the Jaeger Corps.

Second Lieutenant [Karl Ludwig] von Wangenheim to the Linsing Grenadier Battalion.

Second Lieutenant [Karl Friedrich] Bohlen to the Jaeger Corps.

Ensigns [Eugen Benedikt] von Kleist and [Georg] to the Landgraf Regiment.

Ensign [Gottlieb] Greve to the von Buenau Garrison Regiment.

Also twelve non-commissioned officers, three hautboists, two medics, and about 955 privates, including the Jaeger recruits of which there are 224, according to the announcement by the general war commissariat.

Extract of Correspondence, 22 April 1779

(And as I have now not only once more found copies of the lost report of August 11th a.p. among the enclosures of the February 14th, but also the statement from the commandants of the regiments and battalions in America, which was lost at the time, I hereby first of all give the answer to this article that has been postponed hitherto, namely, that their request cannot be considered in any way, as not only is the same amount of money refunded in cash, by means of vacancies for small articles of equipment and other additional items as was refunded in former campaigns, but the small articles of equipment that are sent from here to America are given for the same price as they cost in this country. But the calculation for the vacancies which exist in the company at the commencement of the campaign is no innovation, but rather an old arrangement, which has already been carried out in all former wars, &c.)

As his excellency has decreed the Hessian regiments that are here to be divided among the following brigades, they are so notified:

General Kospath has the Grenadier Battalions.

General von Bose has Donop, Mirbach, and Bose Regiments

Colonel von Wurmb has the Leib, Landgraf, and Prince Charles Regiments.

Mirbach Order Book

August

The 1st - On orders of the colonel, the recruits and clumsy individuals of the four companies of the regiment are to be drilled by Lieutenant Weismueller commencing tomorrow from six to eight o'clock. Sergeant Ritzmann and Corporal Koch are to assist him, and Lieutenant Weismueller and the two non-commissioned officers, except for the most serious requirements, are excused from all other duty. At the same time, the Leib Company is to have its recruits and clumsy individuals drilled by one officer and one non-commissioned officer at the appointed hour.

The inspection of the ball cartridges at the end of each month, as was previously ordered during the month of May, is hoped by the colonel to have been implemented every time, and no less should the uniform accessories be checked at this opportunity, and the results of both are to be reported to the major. The actively of the soldiers is to be sharply observed, so that nothing to incite fighting or other excesses occurs, as the English are stationed nearby, and even more so, however, are the men to be prevented from dealing with them, regardless of what sort of business it might concern.

The colonel has assigned the daily and ordinary duty as follows, pending further orders:

Leib Company
    1) Inspection - one officer

2) Ferry guard - one non-commissioned officer, one drummer, and three privates

3) Guard at the colonel's - three privates

4) Mobile picket to the right of Harlem - four privates   NB - Including a private first class among that number

5) Picket at Lieutenant von Boyneburg's former quarters - one non-commissioned officer and six privates

[Total] - one officer, two non-commissioned officers, one drummer, 16 privates

The four companies at Marston's Wharf

1) Daily - one captain

2) Inspection of the field watch - one officer

3) Field watch - two non-commissioned officers, one drummer, and 21 privates

4) Magazine guard at Marston's Wharf - one non-commissioned officer and twelve privates

5) Guard at Captain Samford's quarters - one non-commissioned officer and four privates

6) Guard at General von Bose - one non-commissioned officer and six privates

7) Guard at the general-in-chief - one non-commissioned officer and six privates

[Total] - one captain, one officer, six non-commissioned officers, one drummer, and 49 privates

For a total sum of one captain, two officers, eight non-commissioned officers, three drummers, and 65 privates

The 2nd - The regiments are to report immediately shortages of ball cartridges, based on sixty rounds per man, and the supply of loose balls on hand.

On orders of the colonel, the companies are to report tomorrow how many cartridges are short, based on sixty rounds per man, and how many loose cartridges are on hand for issue.

Musketeer [Johannes] Wacker of the Leib Company is to be the song leader for Chaplain [Rudolf Reinhard] Virnau.

The 3rd, 4th, and 5th - Nothing.

The 6th - The regiments and battalions are to inspect their munitions frequently and be attentive that no ball ammunition is unnecessarily wasted, also that the loose balls are taken back, so that each time fresh cartridges are issued, the loose balls are turned in.

The 7th - As of this evening, the Leib Company is to provide three men to the picket near the camp at Harlem. This picket is to join with the above mentioned at its post at the same time, remain with the guard throughout the night, and depart again at daybreak.

From the 8th to the 12th - Nothing.

The 13th - The regimental quartermasters of the regiments which worked on the defenses at Laurel Hill are to report at once to the main commissary office in the Broad Street, at New York, where they will receive the money, against receipts, for the period to 1 July, from the engineer. The money for the month of July will also be paid as soon as the pay lists are completed.

All deserters from the rebels, as soon as they come in, are to be escorted to the quarters of His Excellency Lieutenant General von Knyphausen.

The 14th and 15th - Nothing.

The 16th - As the Leib Company no longer provides the picket near Lieutenant von Boyneburg's quarters, the colonel orders that it provide the general and magazine guards near Captain Tomford's quarters, the same as the other companies.

The 17th - The companies are to submit a summary list of the men who worked on Laurel Hill, together with tomorrow's orders. Only those individuals who actually performed work, and not those who were absent at the time, or were sick, are to be considered as having participated.

The 18th and 19th - Nothing.

The 20th - Lord Cathcart is designated as Quartermaster General of the Army, pending further orders.

The companies are to pick up the work money for Laurel Hill from the regimental quartermaster tomorrow, and the colonel orders that the companies pay the men according to the lists submitted, and those men who were at Laurel Hill during the bad

Mirbach Order Book

weather, but did no work, are to receive their share.

The 21st - Nothing.

The 22nd - Because the 44th Regiment has gone to Staten Island, the Hessians are to occupy Redoubt Number 5 with two non-commissioned officers and twenty privates.

The 23rd - The colonel orders that the orderlies on foot are to take their weapons and cartridge pouches with them every time. Also the non-commissioned officers are to report to the staff at the main command at Morrisania the preceding evening.

The 24th - Because the Light Infantry has left Marston's Wharf, the companies are to provide the picket, just as they did previously. Because the 57th Regiment is to march to New York tomorrow, the brigades of von Bose and Wurmb are to occupy Redoubt Number 8 tomorrow, with one officer, three non-commissioned officers, one drummer, and 32 privates.

The 25th - Nothing.

The 26th - As a muster of the regiments is to be held during the first days of the coming week, the colonel orders that the companies prepare two lists at once, according to the style and form as previously done, and complete them by next Sunday morning. All tent, wagon, and regimental servants are to be listed. Dye is to be picked up tomorrow, on Long Island.

Mirbach Order Book

<u>The 27th</u> - In the future no American inhabitants are to be allowed to cross the bridge to this island unless they can show a written pass from the commander of the Hessian Jaeger Corps, or the British Legion. The pass is to contain information that the bearer is to report to General Mathew, or at the Morris house. Also, no one is to be allowed off [the island] without written permission or a pass. Such pass is to be surrendered to the officer commanding the outpost, and is then to be returned to the Morris house the following morning. The officers at the redoubts are not to allow any American inhabitants to move closer to Kingsbridge.

Because the grenadiers march tomorrow, and will take their detachments from the Lossberg huts, and those huts are to be occupied by the regiment, the colonel will inform the lieutenant colonel as to how and in what manner those huts should be occupied.

Pending further orders, the officers at Harlem are to do no duty with the four companies at Marston's Wharf. Lieutenant Weismueller is to perform duty as before.

- - - - - - -

(Copy) - <u>The 28th</u> - Morris house.

The English Commissary of Muster, Porter, desired to muster the Hessian regiments. His Excellency Lieutenant General von Knyphausen has given me the duty of informing General von Bose that

Mirbach Order Book

the von Donop, Mirbach, and Bose Regiments are to submit muster rolls, as they were prepared at the last review, so that the muster master can muster the regiments on the day when he wishes to see them.

The 29th - During the evening, after retreat is fired, no one, whether or not they have a pass, is to cross the bridges on this island, neither coming nor going, but are to be detained until the following morning at reveille. This applies to the American inhabitants, but when dragoons or persons on duty find it necessary to cross, they are not to be detained. At the same time, all regiments and corps are again reminded that during the night, as soon as retreat has occurred, soldiers not on duty are not to leave their camp.

The 30th and 31st - Nothing.

Mirbach Order Book

September

<u>The 1st</u> - Major William Sutherland, commander of the garrison battalion, has been found not guilty of inactivity on the night of the 18th/19th at Paulus Hook, by a military court, and is therefore honorably acquitted.

The general-in-chief has decided to reduce the Jaeger Corps commanded by Lieutenant Colonel Emmerich. The 26th Regiment on the coming Friday is to be divided among the 44th, 23rd, 63rd, 37th, and 64th Regiments.

Sergeant [Henrich] Schade of the Landgraf Regiment is named staff wagonmaster vice the cashiered Wagonmaster Ruppersberg.

The von Mirbach Regiment is to be mustered tomorrow morning at eight, Bose at nine, and Donop at ten.

After Orders

As Commissary of Muster Porter is to muster the troops on Staten Island first on orders of the general-in-chief, the local von Donop, Mirbach, and Bose Regiments are not to be mustered tomorrow, but on the sixth of this month.

<u>The 2nd</u> - All sutlers, from McGowan's Pass to Kingsbridge, are to be informed by the provost guard that all of those who do not have a written license or permission to operate at this place from the regimental or corps commanders where they are in business,

Mirbach Order Book

between now and next Monday, the sixth, are no longer to be tolerated. If they continue to conduct business without permission, their huts are to be torn down, and they are to be turned over, in person, to the provost.

The 3rd - Nothing.

The 4th - Nothing.

The 5th - Tomorrow the von Donop, von Mirbach, and von Bose Regiments are to be mustered.

At eight-thirty tomorrow morning, the four companies are to assemble at Marston's Wharf to be mustered, and at eight o'clock, the Leib Company at the colonel's quarters.

The 6th - Nothing.

The 7th - His Excellency Lieutenant General von Knyphausen orders the regiments to submit two reports each week, on Wednesdays and Saturdays, to him. The columns in which nothing is entered can be omitted.

As woolen trousers are to be worn beginning the end of this month, the colonel orders that the companies take steps to insure that each soldier has a good pair of trousers.

The 8th - The commanding general-in-chief has ordered the regiments and corps, to allow money for the construction of their huts during the coming winter, be paid in the following proportions:

Each English regiment which has completely built

its own huts is to receive twelve pounds sterling per company. Each Hessian Regiment which has completely built its own huts, also, is to receive twenty pounds sterling per company. Those regiments, however, which have only improved old huts or quarters, are to receive half of the allowed sum. Those single companies which are stronger than the others, are to be noted by the regimental commanders when appropriating money, which can be obtained from the quartermaster general office.

The colonel orders that when the companies receive convalescents, they are to be assigned no duty for eight days, and, in so far as possible, insure that they eat no fruit or other highly damaging food initially.

The 9th - Nothing.

The 10th - The von Mirbach company which is at Harlem is not to permit the least damage to the buildings or planks, because these are to be used for barracks.

The 11th - The companies are to submit specific lists of the workers and handymen who worked on the guard tents during the past winter, to the regimental quartermasters, and by each name note how many days each worked.

The 12th - Communications with seamen must be held only at night, from the retreat firing until reveille. Those who cross Kingsbridge during this time, officers as well as others of the Jaeger Corps who wish to leave or return to their corps after retreat, must expect that the guard at Kingsbridge will not let them pass.

The 13th and 14th - Nothing.

The 15th - Colonel [Francis] Lord Rawdon has resigned his position as adjutant general. All the required reports submitted to that department are to be sent to 1st Lieutenant Campbell, deputy adjutant general, pending further orders.

The 16th - The following regiments and corps are to hold themselves in readiness to embark on the shortest notice: The British Grenadiers and Light Infantry, the 7th, 23rd, 33rd, 37th, 54th, and 57th Regiments, the Linsing, Lengercke, Minnigerode, and Graf Grenadier Battalions, as well as 200 foot jaegers, plus the cavalry and infantry of the Queen's Rangers and Fanning's Corps. These regiments and corps are to send their embarkation lists to the adjutant general office on the coming Saturday, according to the accompanying form. The transport ships are to be assigned to those regiments by the agent at the appropriate time.

The 17th - The officers to inspect the guard for the four companies are to take charge of the reserve picket at the same time, and also inspect the hospital. The officers at Harlem are not to perform duty with the four companies at Marston's Wharf, but perform duty

Mirbach Order Book

in Harlem as before.

<u>The 18th</u> - The von Mirbach Regiment is to relieve the watch left behind in the huts near John's house by the Grenadier Brigade, and the grenadiers are to return to their battalions. The regiment can establish the strength of this watch as appropriate. The grenadiers have one non-commissioned officer and sixteen men there at this time.

Werner

One non-commissioned officer and five privates are ordered on this hut watch. The non-commissioned officer and four privates are to remain in the huts on the North River, and one private in the Lossberg huts. The non-commissioned officer is to go back and forth between the huts during the day to insure that nothing is vandalized. The companies are responsible for feeding the men from the mess. The companies are to take the men for this guard who are exhausted, and can do no other duty.

<u>The 19th</u> - The non-commissioned officer in the huts is to be relieved every day, and detached to other guard tours. The privates, however, are to remain [on that guard duty]. The non-commissioned officer is to turn over [the guard at the] huts each time [when he is relieved].

<u>The 20th, 21st, and 22nd</u> - Nothing.

<u>The 23rd</u> - (Further)
<u>Distribution of Recruits to the Regiments</u>

Mirbach Order Book

To Donop - those from Truembach
To Mirbach - those from Wissenbach
To Bose - those from Knyphausen

On the day after tomorrow, 25 September, one officer per brigade and one non-commissioned officer, who can read, from each company are to be sent to pick-up the recruits at New York, of whom it is reported many can not move until they are supplied with uniform accessories. Therefore it is necessary that they arrive by eight o'clock in the morning. Paymaster Schmidt and Captain Martin are to be present at the distribution.   von Cochenhausen

The officer to pick-up the recruits is von Bose.

Volpert

(Copy) - As soon as the instructions from Colonel von Cochenhausen are received that the recruits are to be distributed tomorrow morning, the non-commissioned officers are to insure a timely arrival in New York. Also, the regimental quartermaster or the wagonmaster is to be present with sufficient men, but the men of the baggage guard are not to be used.

Volpert

The general-in-chief has presented the provincial rank of major in His Majesty's (King of England) service to Captain [August] von Wrede of the Hessian Jaeger Corps.

Mirbach Order Book

The 24th - Nothing.

The 25th - All forage is to be delivered to Marston's Wharf and not to the present magazine at Kingsbridge.

The 26th - Nothing.

The 27th - Early tomorrow morning the von Bose Regiment is to march to New York. The time of beginning the march is left to Colonel von Bischhausen's discretion by his excellence. The Artillery Detachment is to remain behind. On orders of his excellence both the von Donop and von Mirbach Regiments are to provide, alternately, a guard of one non-commissioned officer and three privates for Regimental Quartermaster Strube at Fort Knyphausen.

The 28th - The colonel orders that the companies are to begin drilling the recruits, so that they at least learn enough to be able to pull duty, and those companies which are short of officers or non-commissioned officers are to use experienced soldiers to train them.

(Copy) - And it appears from the latest correspondence from Europe that His Serene Highness has been informed that the officers at the regiments and corps here have not been wearing all items exactly prescribed by regulations, the commanders of the regiments, battalions, and corps are to order and insure compliance in the future, so that all officers wear all

Mirbach Order Book

items such as hat, stripes, coat, shirt, and leggings, also sidearms, according to the usual manner and as prescribed by His Serene Highness, and that no other items of clothing be worn.

Knyphausen

The colonel hopes that the officers will adhere to this order.

<u>The 29th</u> - The regimental quartermasters of the regiments which have worked on Laurel Hill can pick up the pay for the work from Engineer Mercyen, who lives in Wall Street.

On the day after tomorrow, 1 October, the wool trousers are to be worn. Therefore the colonel orders that the soldiers who are on duty, and especially those on general guard, wear the prescribed uniform, and do not appear wearing black nor any color but red scarves.

<u>The 30th</u> - Tomorrow the companies are to receive the money for wood-cutting, as well as the hut money from the regimental quartermaster. The money is to be paid from the 1st sergeant to the lowest private, and a report of the payments made to the major by Sunday.

No officer of this company, who has arrived from Europe since 24 September, is to receive the 200 days' forage money.

The corps which has embarked under the command of Lieutenant General Cornwallis is to

Mirbach Order Book

return to land as soon as possible, and take the following positions:

The 7th Regiment to the defenses at Brooklyn; the 23rd and 33rd Regiments to Denyce's house on Long Island.

The 57th Regiment at Sandy Hook remains aboard the ships however, until it receives orders to land.

The Queen's Rangers to Richmond, on Staten Island, and relieve the posts of the 37th Regiment, which is to go immediately to Newtown, because of the many sick.

The Volunteers of Ireland are to land on Staten Island also, and be assigned areas by General Paterson.

The companies of the 44th Regiment, which was ordered to Staten Island, are to join the garrison at Paulus Hook, pending further orders.

The commanding general-in-chief, in orders dated 26 September 1779, has named Colonel Leland of the Guards Brigade to duty as a brigadier general pending further orders.

Mirbach Order Book

October

<u>From the 1st to the 8th</u> - Nothing.

<u>The 9th</u> - The regiments are no longer to send sick individuals to New York, because there is no place to quarter them there. As soon as such are available, it will be announced.

<u>The 10th</u> - Nothing.

<u>The 11th</u> - There is a post of one non-commissioned officer and eighteen privates of the Paromere Corps of Refugees opposite Harlem at Morrisania. If personnel from this post come over on pass, they are to be allowed to pass by the von Mirbach Regiment posts on this side.

<u>The 12th</u> - Nothing.

<u>The 13th</u> - In the future, when pay for wood-cutting is received from the English barracks office, the regimental quartermasters are not to accept this on receipts, but they are to be signed by the commanders of regiments every time.

The regiments and corps can receive their allowance for the royal draft horses from the quartermaster general offices at this time: fourteen pounds of hay and six pounds of corn for each horse.

On orders of the colonel, no recruits who have blue coats are to be selected for the general's watch, but they are to do duty only in the regiment.

<u>The 14th</u> - A report is to be submitted to the Morris house on the coming Saturday as to the number of

Mirbach Order Book

royal wagon servants, wagons, and horses, and the report is to be signed by the commander.

(Copy) - It has already been made known and ordered that for the time being, no more sick individuals can be accepted in the hospital at New York, but such sick persons as the regiment has, who can not be cured by the company medics in the regimental hospital, are to be reported to me. Then one of the non-commissioned officers is to be sent to the hospital administration with the number of sick, so that arrangements for their care can be made, and it will not be necessary to drive the sick around the city looking for accommodations. The companies are to be notified that if a wagon horse is lost, it will not be replaced. Therefore the companies must be very careful with those animals so that they are not overworked nor used, except for regimental service.

C. v. Romrod

From the 15th to the 18th - Nothing.

The 19th - As His Excellency Lieutenant General von Knyphausen has granted permission to dismantle the church in Harlem, the men carrying out that project are not to be prevented from so doing.

Because there are only two officers who can perform duty in the Fourth Company, the colonel orders Lieutenant Berner, for the time being, and until the officers recover, to perform duty with the

Mirbach Order Book

lieutenant colonel, commencing tomorrow.

The 20th - Those regiments actually in camp, which have received no wood from the royal magazine, can request the wood allowance for the six summer month, if they have not already received the allowance from the barracks office. For this reason, the regimental quartermasters are to report to Colonel von Cochenhausen, who will give them further instructions.

The 21st - Captain Diemar's Hussars are attached to the cavalry of Lord Cathcart and pending further orders, are under the command of Lieutenant Colonel [Banastre] Tarleton.

The 22nd and 23rd - Nothing.

The 24th - The regiments, battalions, and corps are to submit a list of invalids according to the usual form, and properly signed, as soon as possible, so that the originals can be sent to Hesse. No others are to be listed except those who are completely incapable of performing duty.

Werner

The 25th - Tomorrow morning, at their convenience, the Leib and Donop Regiments are to march into the city. His Excellency Lieutenant General von Knyphausen requests a written report from the commanders of regiments, battalions, and corps if the last recruit accounts are correct, if they have credits,

Mirbach Order Book

and what amounts have been paid. The Landgraf and Prince Charles Regiments are hereby assigned to the brigade of General von Bose.

The commanding general-in-chief has named Captain [John] Andre of the 54th Regiment as deputy adjutant general, vice Lieutenant Colonel Campbell, who has resigned the position. Therefore all lists and reports are to be sent to Captain Andre.

The 27th - Nothing.

The 28th - Captain-at-arms [Johann Georg] Roddiger, of Major Baurmeister's Company, is promoted to sergeant in place of the deceased Sergeant [Johannes] Giese; Corporal [Johann Georg] Driebe, to captain-at-arms, and Musketeer [Johann Georg] Schaeffer, to corporal. The companies are to compute pay for the recruits according to the normal manner, pay them in cash that which is due, and report to the major by Monday. When the recruits arrived in New York the regimental quartermaster paid each, one schilling. If this has not yet been paid, it can be paid at this time.

There is no longer to be a guard in the huts on the North River, but each day a private is to watch those, of the Lossberg Regiment.

The 29th - On orders of General Mathew, no guard is to be given the countersign except under special necessity, and on orders of headquarters at Morris house.

Mirbach Order Book

Headquarters, Denyce's House on Long Island, 25 October 1779

The commanding general-in-chief has made the following assignments of winter quarters for the troops for this winter.

York Island

The Guard Brigade, Prince Charles and Hereditary Prince Regiments, and the Hessian Jaeger Corps at Laurel Hill.

The von Mirbach Regiment in the area of McGowan's Pass.

The 64th Regiment in the quarters on the East River occupied by the 7th Regiment last winter.

The Loyal Americans cantoned from Bloomingthal to John's house.

The von Bose Regiment in the quarters on the North River occupied by the 63rd Regiment last winter.

The Royal Artillery, the four Hessian Grenadier Battalions, the 42nd and 54th Regiments, and Skinner's 2nd Battalion at New York and Bowery Lane.

Long Island

The Light Infantry and British Grenadiers in the huts at Jamaica.

The 17th Dragoon Regiment at Hempstedt.

The 23rd and 80th Regiments in the huts at Bedford.

The 33rd Regiment in huts at Denyce's House.

Mirbach Order Book

The 37th Regiment at Newtown.

The 76th Regiment cantoned in Brooklyn until new barracks are finished in the new defenses.

More on Long Island

The Leib Regiment is to occupy the cantonments of the 76th Regiment as soon as the barracks in the new defenses are finished.

The von Donop Regiment to Bushwick

DeLancey's 3rd Battalion and the King's American Regiment at Lloyd's Neck.

Lord Cathcart's Legion at Jericho.

The Guards and Pioneers in their last winter's quarters.

Staten Island

The 7th Regiment in the huts which the 26th Regiment occupied last winter.

The 63rd Regiment at the Flagstaff.

The Landgraf Regiment in the huts which the Graf Grenadier Regiment occupied last winter.

Skinner's 1st Battalion in their present huts.

The 4th Battalion in the huts near Skinner's 1st Battalion.

The regiments are to receive their further orders as to when they are to enter their respective quarters, and every possible help and assistance is to be given for building their huts.

Hutchinson
Deputy Adjutant General

Mirbach Order Book

<u>The 30th</u> - The Landgraf Regiment is to march to New York tomorrow morning and enter the camp occupied by the Hereditary Prince Regiment.

The corps which have orders to enter huts in this district, can report to the assistant engineer, Lieutenant Sproule, and receive the necessary tools to build huts.

The colonel orders that all recruits belonging to the regiment be ready at the flag at eight o'clock tomorrow morning to take an oath on the same. Ensign [Heinrich Friedrich] Lange and Free Corporal [Jacob] Biskamp are ordered to be present.

At the designated time, the auditor of the Landgraf Regiment is to be present at the flag.

As Sergeant [Cyriacus Ludwig] Schultz as of next Monday is to assume the duty as 1st sergeant, the colonel orders Free Corporal [Johann Georg] Meurer to assume the duty of regimental clerk from now on.

As soon as the English Grenadiers leave the house in Harlem, it is to be reported to the colonel, because the regiment is to occupy it immediately and send the sick individuals there.

His Excellency Lieutenant General von Knyphausen, has assigned Lieutenant Colonel [Ferdinand Heinrich] von Schuler, of the von Ditfurth Regiment, as commander of the vacant von Minnigerode Grenadier Battalion, pending further approval of His Serene Highness. The regiments, battalions, and corps are to pay the credits from the yearly four Reichstaler uniform accessories money to their non-commissioned officers and privates immediately, and ensure that no other items which really are not uniform accessories are charged to the troops. Should such be discovered, however, it must be changed, and in every case the cash be paid out. Then, the new accessories accounts for 1779 are to begin, and continued until the next accounting and disbursement of credits to the end of 1780.

Werner
Brigade Major

Extract of Correspondence from His Serene Highness Dated, Weissenstein, 21 June 1779

Recently I have seen the uniform accessories accounts, in which, with the greatest astonishment and displeasure, I saw that the two grenadiers, Schroeder and Bauer, were mistreated in a seriously punishable manner by the captains, so that all the 9 December 1771 uniform regulations and orders given to the regiments have been ignored, and that Grenadier Schroeder, in an unheard of manner, had to enter the accounting for the repair of his weapon in the uniform accessories book.

Such unpardonable misconduct by an officer is against my wishes and merit's the most severe reprisal.

(The Lieutenant General must have the matter very strictly enquired into by a commission that is to be appointed, and to be presided over by Colonel von Cochenhausen, and to be assisted by an expert accountant, and this commission is to enquire into the account for small articles of equipment, and how it has been managed, as well as into other similar ones that may be found - although I trust not - to discover the regiment and captains of the companies to which Grenadiers Schroeder and Bauer belong, and to hear the captain's justifications; but even then the whole matter is to be notified to me for further decision. In the two above-mentioned accounts for small articles of equipment, it appears that a deduction was made for black gaiters and same charged to the two Grenadiers' account, that very few small articles of equipment had been given to them for several years, not even for the sum of 4 Reichstalers that was granted every year for that purpose, that the balance in their favor was carried forward from one year to another, consequently that same was not paid out to them in cash at the end of the year, which would have been the right thing to do. The Lieutenant General must therefore issue very strict orders to all the captains and commandants of the regiments concerning this matter, namely, that nothing whatsoever may be put down in a non-commissioned officer's and private's account-book for small articles of equipment, except small articles of equipment, therefore nothing whatsoever that comes under the heading of large articles of equipment, and same must be put down to their account at the price paid for them; further, that nothing may be deducted from a man's allowance or any other douceurs he may have received for any reason, or under any pretext whatsoever, otherwise the punishment that shall certainly be meted out will be very severe, consequently, that he cannot be called to account for anything except the 4 Reichstalers that have been granted for small articles of equipment, that any possible balance in his favour (but this will fall away of itself, provided the necessary small articles of equipment are duly given to him) is to be paid out to him at the end of March every year, at which time the yearly settlement takes place, but that the amount which the companies then owe for small articles of equipment is to fall on nobody but the captain who has had the company until the end of March, without there being any hope of his ever having it refunded; thus neither balance in favor nor money owing from the year that is past may be carried forward to April, or the new year for any reason whatever, so that neither the one thing nor the other can any longer exist at the commencement of the new year, consequently that no debts can be put down on the account of a new captain of a company by his predecessor, should the company have become vacant at the end of March, by means of transfer or other reason, neither can he be called to repay same.

Mirbach Order Book

(My opinion concerning all this has already been notified to the Lieutenant General under the date November 11th a.p., as well as that the debts the private contracts every year by paying out more than the 4 Reichstalers that are intended for small articles of equipment, are to be defrayed out of the money set aside for recruiting purposes and vacancies.

(The complaints that have been sent in from the regiments to the effect, that the captains of companies had to add such a considerable sum of money to the 4 Reichstalers that had been set aside for small articles of equipment, cannot be reconciled with the large amount of money that is owing to the men, which has been seen from various company-accounts, and quite lately from those belonging to the former von Wutgenau, which I have come across. Upon the whole it is incomprehensible, how the companies can have such a large balance in their favor, and that the Hoepfner company has the sum of 273 Reichstalers to its credit, after deducting the debts from February 1st, 1776, until the end of January 1777. It becomes evident from this, that the men have hardly received any small articles of equipment or at least very few, and that they themselves have been compelled to provide same out of their allowance; but this is contrary to my intentions, and therefore be emphatically forbidden.

(I rely most thoroughly upon the Lieutenant

Mirbach Order Book

General, that every conceivable measure be taken in order that my object can be gained, all abuses hindered and put an end to, and that the bad results that are otherwise inevitable, may be prevented.)

<u>Orders, Headquarters Denyce's,
29 October 1779</u>

The troops from Rhode Island are assigned as follows, pending further orders:

The 22nd, 38th, and 43rd Regiments at Saltuchet under the command of Major General Schmidt.

The Hessian Ditfurth, Huyn, and Buenau Regiments to Huntington under the command of General von Lossberg.

The two Ansbach battalions into the barracks of the 54th Regiment to join the 37th Regiment at Newtown.

The Prince of Wales American Volunteers and New England Loyalists to Lloyd's Neck. The troops proceeding to Lloyd's Neck, Huntington, and Saltuchet are to travel next Monday in their transport ships to Whitestone, under escort of *Hercules*, where they are to await another convoy, whereupon the British and Hessians are to land. Captain Savage, deputy paymaster general, is to supply wagons to the troops for transporting their baggage.

Skinner's 2nd Battalion is to go to Jerusalem on Long Island as soon as the major general finds it convenient.

The rest of the army can enter its respective winter quarters at its convenience.

The regimental quartermasters of those corps entering huts can obtain the following tools from the engineer's storehouse, on the wharf behind the coffeehouse:

Sixteen large axes, twelve shovels, twelve rakes, eight pickaxes, and one barrel of nails.

The British Guards, Grenadiers, Light Infantry, 80th Regiment, and the Jaegers can receive a double portion.

Each corps from Rhode Island is to have a house in New York assigned for its heavy baggage.

His Excellency Lieutenant von Knyphausen orders the Hereditary Prince Regiment to march to Laurel Hill as quickly as possible, and General Mathew orders the Landgraf Regiment to enter the camp in the city, pending further orders.

The provincial troops at Lloyd's Neck are to send their reports to Brigadier DeLancey.

                              Hutchinson
                        Deputy Adjutant General

<u>Orders, Headquarters, D.H.,</u>
<u>30 October 1779</u>

The general-in-chief has made the following changes in the dispersal of the troops from Rhode

Mirbach Order Book

Island:
The 22nd, 38th, and von Huyn Regiments are to debark next Wednesday at Yellow Hook and enter camp there, under Major General Schmidt, pending further orders. The 43rd and von Ditfurth Regiments are to land the same day at Brooklyn, and march on land to Huntington, under the command of Brigadier General Leland.

The Prince of Wales Volunteers and Loyal New England provincials are to march on land the same day, to Lloyd's Neck.

The 57th Regiment is to join the three regiments at Yellow Hook, under the command of Major General Schmidt.

The Volunteers of Ireland are to return to Staten Island. The companies of the 82nd Regiment are to camp from Brooklyn as far as Red Hook.

The von Buenau Regiment is to proceed to Staten Island and occupy the huts which the Landgraf Regiment used, under the command of Brigadier General Paterson.

Hutchinson
Deputy Adjutant General

<u>The 31st</u> - the huts of the Landgraf Regiment are to be given to the English Guards.

On order of the colonel, the regiment is to assemble with the flags and cannons tomorrow

Mirbach Order Book

morning at precisely nine o'clock at the huts which the two companies of the von Lossberg Regiment have occupied, and occupy the new emplacements in which the huts are to be placed this winter. Lieutenant Berner is to point out the place tomorrow morning. One non-commissioned officer and six privates are to remain in camp to guard the huts.

Mirbach Order Book

November

<u>The 1st</u> - When a fire alarm sounds, the regiments and corps are to assemble under arms before their huts.

P.S. The huts which have been occupied by the von Lossberg Regiment can be used by the von Mirbach Regiment for building winter huts.

<u>The 2nd</u> - <u>Orders, Headquarters on Long Island</u>

The general-in-chief has ordered the quartermaster guard to deliver part of the blankets, gloves, cloth for long trousers and fittings, shirts, linen for shirts as well as for fittings, ticking for trousers, shoes, shoe soles, and thick woolen stockings, which came from England, to the British and Hessian soldiers. Those regiments which receive the items must pay for them according to the price which has not yet arrived from England. The regiments and corps which wish to receive those items are to submit a strength list, signed by the commander, to the quartermaster general office by the tenth of this month. The provincials are to receive an equal proportion from the inspector of the general store.

Hutchinson
Deputy Adjutant General

<u>The 3rd</u> - Nothing.

<u>The 4th</u> -   <u>Orders, New York</u>

The invalids listed by the regiments, battalions, and corps in the invalids lists, are to be prepared to embark on the shortest notice. Lieutenant General von Knyphausen orders that their accounts be correct, and that all credits be paid in cash.

The requested, original lists must be attested by the regimental surgeon, and he is to submit an abstract as soon as possible.

Werner
Brigade Major

<u>The 5th</u> -   Orders, New York

His Excellence Lieutenant General von Knyphausen repeats the often given order of 9 October concerning the cash payment of those accounts the non-commissioned officers and privates have coming from the yearly 4 Reichstaler uniform accessories money, through the end of 1778, and that no other items except those belonging to the uniform accessories accounts are to be entered in the accounts.

His excellence points out to all the commanders the correspondence from His Serene Highness, dated 27 June 1779, that the accounting for the uniform accessories, according to the already given order, money credits of the non-commissioned officers and privates through the end of 1778, are to be paid only in cash, and nothing in the uniform accessories is to be considered during the past period, in lieu of cash, even if so requested.

<u>The 6th</u> - The von Mirbach Regiments is to receive

bedding and candles on the coming Thursday at the barracks office, at nine o'clock in the morning. If the regiment is lacking some hand tools, and if it wishes cooking pots, if the regimental quartermaster submits a list of those items, they can be obtained with the bedding.

The 7th - P.S. Colonel von Romrod is to be given positive information concerning the emplacement this afternoon.

At nine o'clock tomorrow morning, the regiment is to be prepared to march to occupy the huts of the Lossberg Regiment. From each of the two detached companies and the one at the Mill, one officer is to have the inspection each day. As to how guard mount is to be held, orders are to be given tomorrow. Baurmeister's Company is to remain in place until all sick individuals are removed from the Mill. That company is to bring the flags to the colonel's quarters.

Orders, New York, 7 November 1779

Distribution of brigades by Lieutenant General von Knyphausen:

The Grenadier Battalion of Major General von Kospoth, in New York.

Hereditary Prince, Prince Charles, and the Mirbach Regiments, and the Jaegers -- Major General von Bose, at New York and McGowan's Pass.

Donop Regiment at Bushwick, Leib Regiment at Hallet's Cove, but move later to Brooklyn, and the

Mirbach Order Book

Bose Regiment on the North River, three miles from New York -- General von Lossberg.

Lossberg Regiment in New York and Buenau Regiment on Staten Island -- Colonel von Hachenberg.

The invalids must be ready to come here as soon as ordered, because the English adjutant general office will announce the embarkation only four days prior to boarding, and from the time the information reaches the regiments and corps, they must then definitely be here by the announced time.

<u>Order, Headquarters, 7 November 1779</u>

Because of the high prices for food and other articles, the general-in-chief orders that the troops hold their lists for 165 days' forage money in readiness. As soon as the troops enter winter quarters, those lists are to be forwarded and the money paid out at once. Officers of absent regiments entitled to this money must so notify the quartermaster general.

As soon as the huts for the regiments are finished and ready for occupancy, and the regimental commanders have submitted reports to the quartermaster general, the authorized money for building the huts is to be paid out at once.

Lieutenant Willington is designated as paymaster for the non-commissioned officers and privates of the absent regiments, vice Lieutenant Green, who is returning to his regiment. Mr. McKay is designated assistant barracks master for the 32nd Regiment,

Mirbach Order Book

vice Lieutenant Carlston, who has resigned that position.

Hutchinson
Deputy Adjutant General

<u>The 8th</u> - Nothing.

<u>The 9th</u> - The 64th Regiment is to enter winter quarters today.

<u>Order, New York, 9 November 1779</u>

The uniform accessories accounting for the invalids through the end of 1779 is to be prepared. Pay and provisions however, are to be furnished to them from the date of departure for three months. The pay is to be delivered to Captain Reichel, and War Cashier Schmidt is responsible for the provisions they will take. All the regiments and corps are to submit the personnel lists for compilation of the 165 days' forage money list to Colonel von Cochenhausen.

Werner

<u>The 10th</u> - A picket of one non-commissioned officer and six privates is to be posted in the defenses by the Negroes' huts on the East River every day, taking and maintaining the post as usual.

<u>The 11th</u> -   <u>Order, New York</u>

His Excellence Lieutenant General von Knyphausen awaits a written report from each regiment and corps if the troops have been paid the

Mirbach Order Book

credits from the uniform accessories monies owed to them to the end of 1778, as ordered. The honorable regiments and corps belonging to the brigade are to send in the above-mentioned reports here as soon as possible, by order of General Bose.

The 12th - Every Saturday morning the regiments are to send in a list of the royal wagons and horses and their condition to the royal wheelwright near Fort Knyphausen. The honorable regiment are to send in a list of the deserters here, whenever they get any, and the original will then be forwarded to Lieutenant [sic] von Knyphausen from here.

The honorable regiment is to furnish a picket near the North River consisting of one non-commissioned officer and six privates dating from today, and same will take its position near the house which is between the English Grenadiers' area and the John's house. Captain Reichhold is to assign the location.

The 13th- The so often given order about stealing fences, is repeated most strenuously by the colonel, and the first individual who is caught is to be severely punished by running the gauntlet. This provides opportunity to announce that Mr. Apthorp has an English guard on his property, and if anyone is caught trying to steal his fences, is to be brought to the staff watch at once.

The 14th - The message sent to General Mathew by General von Bose, concerning the forage for captains, has been received. The captains of the regiments and corps have the right to receive forage like those who have received it for some time, and it is only necessary for them to report to Commissary Whier.

As the barracks utensils have now been received, and distributed to the companies, it is their responsibility to guard against the loss of blankets and tools, such as axes and saws, because the companies are responsible, and they must pay for anything missing. Mattresses are not to be sent to the hospital, but only blankets. The woolen stockings are to be distributed to the soldiers immediately. During the construction and repair, the companies are to work on only one at a time, and everyone is to work on it. Wood necessary for the repairs can be obtained at DeLancey's woods, but everything must be done in a proper manner, and a non-commissioned officer is to be sent each time. Wood for fires can be obtained at the same time, but not by individuals. Instead, an officer with the necessary detail of men is to be detached each day to cut and measure it, for which latter action further orders are to be forthcoming.

The 15th - As a guard of one non-commissioned officer and six privates is to be provided at the general-in-chief's country home by the 64th Regiment, commencing tomorrow, the guard detail is to be changed.

(Copy) <u>Order, New York, 13 November 1779</u>

Mirbach Order Book

To my 9 November request to the general-in-chief, to permit more frequent visits to the widely scattered sick individuals, due to the locations of the regimental cantonments, and also, when a surgeon's assistant was sick and another had to visit two regiments on horseback, one ration [for the horse] is to be allowed. This was authorized and an order concerning it is to be sent to the general commissary, Whier, but with the understanding that this is an exception due to circumstances, and is not to be seen as a right.

Knyphausen

The 16th - The caretaker of the DeLancey woods has complained to the colonel, that the soldiers have cut measured wood as well as the wood which was meant to be cut for building the huts, although this is in direct opposition to the colonel's direct orders. Therefore, no company soldiers are to be sent into the woods to cut wood for building huts unless accompanied by a non-commissioned officer, and still less are they to take prepared wood. Therefore, the commanders of companies are to strictly adhere to this order.

The 17th - The Mirbach Regiment is to have duty in the city in the future, exactly as the other regiments, which are on duty, in 48 hour tours.

Commencing today, one officer, two non-commissioned officers, one drummer, and 25 privates

Mirbach Order Book

are to be assigned to the reserve picket. When an alarm occurs, they are to assemble at the camp guard and await further orders. The officer of this picket is to report to the officer of the day prior [to going on duty], and then both to the staff officer, whether or not guard mount is held.

Those officers who have inspection of the various camps are to be sent into arrest at once if they are not present when the staff officer inspects. No captain nor subaltern, nor private is to go into the city without leave. If soldiers go into the city, they are to be orderly at all times, for which the company commander is to be held responsible. All guards are to be inspected during the morning by the company commander, and all officers are to be present.

The 18th - The corps under the command of General Mathew is to fire a *feu de joie* tomorrow afternoon at five o'clock for the success of the royal arms in Georgia. The regiments are to be ready at the designated time, and make the best possible appearance. The three cartridges for the firing are to be prepared by the regiments from the live rounds. The place, where the regiments are to conduct the firing, is to be determined tomorrow.

The regiments, as ordered, are to be as clean and polished as possible. Each soldier is to wear a clean white shirt. The officers are to be uniformly dressed. For the three rounds for firing, the balls are to be taken

Mirbach Order Book

from the ammunition and saved. Recruits can be used at the camp guard at McGowan's Pass, and in the Mill, also. The Leib, Major Wilmowsky's, and Major Baurmeister's Companies can each send one recruit to the watch. The others are to be separated from the staff watch, under arms. No soldiers are to bear arms, who have not fired. Building of huts is to cease tomorrow, but the companies which can not be under arms, nor on other duty, can continue construction.

The Artillery is to be prepared for this firing, also, and have three blank rounds available.

<u>The 19th</u> - The von Mirbach Regiment is to be directly behind General von Bose's quarters at precisely four o'clock this afternoon, and close on the left wing of the Jaegers. Lieutenant Colonel von Wurmb is to give the regiment further instructions. The von Mirbach Regiment fires after the Jaegers. The cannons remain in camp, and the regiment is to leave a small guard behind. The colonel orders the companies to form immediately upon receipt of this, and to assemble at three o'clock at the flags. All camp guards are to be maintained. The soldiers are to place the three rounds for firing in their pockets.

<u>Headquarters, New York, 14 November 1779</u>

In order to establish the necessary economy in distributing forage and fodder, the commander-in-chief orders that no officer is to receive forage and fodder from any place, except that place where he is.

Mirbach Order Book

If officers are sent to New York when sick, they are to submit their name to Doctor North, Superintendent General. Every week a report from the deputy adjutant general and the superintendent general is to be submitted to the general commissary listing the names of officers in New York, because of duty requirements, and of the sick officers so that their receipt of forage can be justified.

When officers come to New York, and must remain for a prolonged period because of duty assignments, and desire quarters, they are to submit their name and business purpose to the adjutant general office.

The commander-in-chief hopes that the officers, on their honor, will not draw more than the authorized and required moneys and forage for their horses. The commissary general and the barracks master are to submit a list at once of those persons who, on direct orders, receive forage and fodder, on which it is to be noted who issued the order, and when it was issued.

The commander-in-chief orders that no officer who does not belong to the garrison, and who is not sick, is to take quarters in the city, except general officers and those who have permission of the general-in-chief, or the commander of the garrison. Therefore, the barracks master general is to submit a list to the commander immediately of those persons who have permission to have headquarters in the city, with the

Mirbach Order Book

name of the individual giving the order, and when the order was given.   Hutchinson
Deputy Adjutant General

Order, Headquarters, New York
8 November 1779

His excellence the general-in-chief herewith notifies the army of the success of the royal arms in Georgia. The French troops and the rebellious colonies stormed the city of Savannah with their full strength. Due to the gallant and good disposition of the troops under the command of the British general, they were completely driven back. His excellence the general-in-chief is not yet familiar with further details of this success, but is assured that the report is based on fact.

The 20th - On orders of General Mathew, every man of his command is to receive an extra ration of rum because of the success in Georgia. They may receive this at supply.

Guard mount is to be held at ten o'clock in the morning. All guards are to assemble prior to that time, by hut number two, on the area of the street to the left of the Leib Company.

The 21st - It has been ordered previously, and strictly forbidden to chop wood in the Apthorp woods, and to take down fences. It appears however, as if it will not cease, and daily continues, and therefore

Apthorp's complaints to the colonel are endless. Therefore, he orders for the last time, that no soldier should misunderstand that anyone taking the least thing from Apthorp's property in countervention thereto, who is caught, is to run the gauntlet twelve times, and the company commander who does not stress this order to his troops, is to be punished with two days' arrest.

The companies at Marston's Wharf are to insure that a fireplace is built into the guard huts at that place.

The 22nd - The regiments are to report the number of huts for which boards for doors and windows, hinges, and glass are especially needed.

The colonel orders that officers on wood detail are to report to him on the day prior to going on duty.

The 23rd, 24th, and 25th - Nothing.

The 26th - General Mathew orders that no one from the regiments under his command, that is, the English Guards, Hereditary Prince, Prince Charles, and Mirbach Regiments, the Jaeger Corps, Althouse's Company, the Pioneers, and Artillery, go to New York without a written pass from the commander of his regiment. Those apprehended without a pass are to be arrested at once, and delivered to their own regiment.

The colonel orders that as the bakers have not baked for the regiment this month, the penny for the

Mirbach Order Book

bakers' pay is not to be deducted from the soldiers for this month.

According to the above order, no one, non-commissioned officers or privates, is to go into the city without a written pass from the colonel. The companies are to complete the passes and send them here to be signed. If it is necessary for a non-commissioned officer with a number of privates to have leave in the city, the pass can be valid for more than the one non-commissioned officer.

In order to prevent unnecessary interruption when bringing wood for the regiment, and disputes with the caretaker of DeLancey's woods, the subsequent receipts are to have two seals, one from the mentioned caretaker, and the other from the regimental quartermaster granting the authorization, which is to be shown to the mentioned caretaker by the commanding officer or non-commissioned officer, every time wood is to be picked up. The seal must be very sharp and clean, and not be lost, otherwise the oficer is to be punished with two days' arrest, and the non-commissioned officer with 48 hours in the stocks. The mentioned seal is to be returned to the regimental quartermaster after use, and he must be told at that time how many wagon loads of wood were cut. No other wood is to be cut, except what the caretaker designates, and of that amount, the stem end as well as the other measurable wood may be loaded, but not higher than three-fourths full.

The 27<u>th</u> - The regiments and corps are to submit a list of soldiers who belong to [General John] Burgoyne's army, and are now in their regiments.

The 28<u>th</u> and 29<u>th</u> - Nothing.

The 30<u>th</u> - All guards are to asemble at the designated places tomorrow morning at ten o'clock. The companies are to remain clean and polished at all times.

The companies at Marston's Wharf, as well as the Leib Company and Major Wilmowsky's Company, are to assign three more men in their camp guard, who are to man such posts as are to be designated later.

Mirbach Order Book

December

The 1st - Nothing.

The 2nd - The regiments are to submit a list for the 165 days' forage money to the quartermaster general, who is then to make payment at once. The regiments are to beat tattoo at eight o'clock, commencing today.

The 3rd - Regimental quartermasters of the regiments and corps are to report at the quarters of Captain Faye of the Royal Artillery, near Fort Knyphausen, tomorrow morning at eleven o'clock, in order to get materials for their huts.

The 4th As the designated invalids are to embark at the Wood Wharf in New York by Monday, the colonel orders all of them to be brought to the baggage house tomorrow, and then to be taken to the place for embarkation by a non-commissioned officer on the following day. The invalids are to be paid through the end of February.

Orders, Headquarters, New York

Those regiments which have prisoners with the rebels and wish to send money or uniform items to them, must submit a list of them to Mr. Loring, commissary of prisoners.

Regimental Orders

In the event of an alarm, the companies are to assemble before their huts and cantonments, with weapons, and await further orders. The soldiers in the huts at McGowan's Pass are to march at once to the

Mirbach Order Book

flags, and the reserve picket to McGowan's Pass.

The 5th - Nothing.

The 6th - The colonel orders that the officer of the picket is to inspect the hospital each day, and make his report at parade in the morning.

The companies are to be supplied with wood sleds as in the previous year.

<u>Order, New York, 6 December 1779</u>

On orders of His Excellency Lieutenant General von Knyphausen, Ensign Weissenborn, as well as all the Wissenbach recruits, are to be prepared to proceed to this city on the shortest notice, in order to embark with the von Huyn Regiment.

P.S. The order has been issued to the embarking regiments that the officers should obtain provisions for themselves for several weeks, and if the expedition does not take place, the cost of the provisions is to be repaid to them.

<u>Regimental After Orders</u>

1st Sargeant Weissenborn, assigned to this regiment, is graciously promoted to ensign in the Wissenbach Regiment by His Serene Highness. Commencing today, the recruits are not to be assigned to any external duties.

The 1st sergeants are to submit a list tomorrow morning, stating where the absent recruits are to be found. Due to the promotion of Ensign Weissenborn, the company is to ask at the commissariat when he is

Mirbach Order Book

to be transferred from the regiment, so that his accounts can be brought up to date.

The 7th - As it has been learned that the troops at this post have been cutting down and burning the fruit trees, General Mathew wished the regimental and corps commanders would order this to cease, and that the Jaegers, in particular, better protect trees and not chop any more down.

The 8th -   Order, New York

From the following listed regiments, a detachment of chasseurs is to be taken, consisting of three officers, eleven non-commissioned officers, two drummers, and 100 men. From:

1) The Leib Regiment - one non-commissioned officer and nine privates.

2) The Landgraf Regiment - the same.

3) The Hereditary Prince Regiment - one officer, one non-commissioned officer, one drummer, and nine privates.

4) The Prince Charles Regiment - one officer, one non-commissioned officer, and ten privates.

5) The von Ditfurth Regiment - one non-commissioned officer and ten privates.

6) The von Donop Regiment - one non-commissioned officer and eight privates.

7) The von Lossberg Regiment - one non-commissioned officer and six privates.

8) The von Mirbach Regiment - one non-commissioned officer and eight privates.
9) The von Bose Regiment - one non-commissioned officer and nine privates.
10) The von Huyn Regiment - one officer, one non-commissioned officer, one drummer, and eleven privates.
11) The von Buenau Regiment - one non-commissioned officer and eleven privates.
TOTAL - Three officers, eleven non-commissioned officers, two drummers, and 100 privates.

Second Lieutenant [Ernst Wilhelm] von Anderson of the Hereditary Prince Regiment, whose date of rank is 26 February 1776, and who served previously with the chasseurs, is ordered to do so again. The other two officers, second lieutenants, one each from the Prince Charles Regiment and the Huyn Regiment, have more recent dates of rank. For the soldiers, dependable and robust men from Hesse are to be chosen, and no foreigners, and as many as possible are to be taken from those who served in the chasseur corps previously. They are to remain with their regiments for the present, but must be ready to assemble at the Common Place in New York on the shortest notice. If part of the von Huyn Regiment is to be embarked, those chosen for this assignment are to be sent here. The von Ditfurth Regiment is to send its

Mirbach Order Book

men here immediately, as should the von Lossberg Regiment.

Pay for the men to the end of December 1779 is to be given to the non-commissioned officers.

Regimental Order

As mentioned in the above order, the Lieutenant Colonel's Company is to designate a competent non-commissioned officer, and the companies, when possible, are to take men who were assigned to this command in the previous year, or if that is not possible, men who can be relied upon.

Order, New York, 9 December

The Carlshaven operating committee has ordered that no officer or military person is to be given credit nor allowed to assign extraordinary amounts, unless the credit or assignment is approved and signed by the commander. Therefore, His Excellence Lieutenant General von Knyphausen herewith announces and orders that it is not necessary for the commanders to accept (such assignments which they have not agreed to and signed when extra ordinary money is paid out, nor need they deduct them from the officers' money.)

The regiments are to submit a list of non-commissioned officers, drummers, and privates of those individuals selected for the chasseur corps as soon as possible, in the same manner as that submitted by the Prince Charles Regiment. Among the officers and privates, no one is to be included who has

Mirbach Order Book

assigned part of his pay to Hesse.

Werner

<u>The 9th</u> - Nothing.

<u>The 10th</u> - The companies are responsible for providing the troops ordered to the chasseurs with two good shirts, one pair of wool trousers, leggings, and shoes, and to send a pair of shoe soles along with them so that they can be maintained for several months, and their uniforms must be mended and in good repair.

<u>Order, New York, 7 December 1779</u>

As a convoy sails from here for Georgia in a few days, those officers belonging to the regiments at that place are to submit their name to the office of the adjutant general, so as to make the necessary arrangements for the trip.

<u>Order, New York, 8 December 1779</u>

The regiments and corps are to submit a list of their ammunition shortages. Brigade Major [Frederick] McKenzie is named deputy adjutant general.

Lieutenant Colonel Tumbel of the York Volunteers is to take command over the officers and privates belonging to provisional corps embarking for Georgia.

<u>Garrison Order, 10 December 1779</u>

The report concerning the horses to be embarked, which was submitted by the quartermaster general, can not be understood, that more than are absolutely necessary for duty, can be embarked. The general-in-chief allows the corps to leave their horses behind and to receive forage, but only for those in their possession. It is to be announced when the horses for sale to the quartermaster general yard can be delivered.

<u>The 11th</u> -   <u>Order, New York</u>

All invalids and widows are to embark for Europe next Monday morning at ten o'clock, in the following order:

The 26th Regiment at Whitehall.

British invalids at the Hay Wharf.

Hessians and Ansbach invalids at the Wood Wharf.

The women for England.

The women going to Ireland at Roomingstep.

<u>The 12th</u> - Nothing.

<u>The 13th</u> - Regimental Surgeon Hencke of the Jaeger Corps is to attend the sick of the regiment, pending further orders.

<u>The 14th</u> - Nothing.

Mirbach Order Book

The 15th - Order, New York

The staff officers and officers belonging to the staff who send horses on board may receive forage for their horses on the trip, from the general commissary.

Ten head of sheep, plus the necessary forage, are to be delivered to each regiment for the trip. Corps and detachments are to receive provisions based on their strength.

The 16th - The watch is to be discontinued pending further orders. If a formation is to be held, the companies are to announce it.

Ensign Weissenborn is to be buried at three o'clock tomorrow afternoon.

The 17th - Nothing.

The 18th - General Mathew has named Captain Richardson his supernumerary adjutant pending further orders, and all his orders are to be respected as coming from General Mathew.

Order, New York

The chasseur detachment is to assemble day after tomorrow, the 20th, here at New York, at the Common Place at twelve o'clock noon, in order to be embarked. The ship called *Ann*, on which the chasseur detachment and Captain Hanger are to embark, lies in the East River at the Crown Wharf.

Those of the Hereditary Prince, Prince Charles, and Mirbach Regiments are to insure that they arrive here at the designated time.   Werner

Mirbach Order Book

Those men selected for the chasseur detachment are to assemble at nine o'clock tomorrow morning at the Colonel's Company. The men are to be paid through the end of December, for which Corporal Kilian is responsible.

<u>The 19th</u> - As it will not be possible in the future for the privates to haul their wood in the wagons, the colonel orders that the companies are responsible for completing the wood sleighs as soon as possible. As by the already issued order of His Excellency General von Knyphausen, the Wissenbach recruits are to be embarked at New York at nine o'clock tomorrow morning, the colonel orders that Lieutenant von Biesenrodt and the recruits assemble at seven o'clock tomorrow morning at the Colonel's Company in order to march, so as to be at the Common Place near Captain Bauer's quarters, at precisely nine o'clock. A list is to be given to the regimental quartermaster as to the period for which the recruits have been given pay and provisions.

<u>Order, Headquarters, New York,</u>
<u>19 December 1779</u>

Those officers who have left horses behind, are to give their name to the general commissary so that forage can be delivered for them.

<u>The 20th</u> - The regiments and corps are to submit a list at once of their wagons and horses, their condition, and if usable or not. Complaints have been

Mirbach Order Book

received that the spruce beer delivered to the regiments is very bad. Therefore, the regiments may receive a double amount of spruce beer, in lieu of the amount of the old one.

As the chasseurs and Wissenbach recruits are no longer with the regiment, the colonel orders that the companies, according to their strength, reduce the messes to thirteen or fourteen.

In the future it is not necessary during bad weather for the captain of the day to report to the colonel, but only during good weather. The colonel herewith gives the wagon master the strictest orders to take all the unshod horses into the city tomorrow, and not to come back until the wagons are repaired, and the horses shod. He is also to insure that those of Major von Wilmowsky are trade for two good wagon horses.

The 21st - Those regiments and corps which have finished building their huts are to return the construction tools to the engineer store. Those which have officer huts to build, however, can keep the tools. However, the regimental quartermasters are responsible for them, and must return them as soon as finished.

The 22nd - The regimental and corps wagons are to be prepared, and also the necessary horses and harnesses are to be put in a condition so that they can move out on the shortest notice.

Mirbach Order Book

Order, Headquarters, New York
21 December 1779

The regiments and corps which are to embark are to take the following proportions of wagons and harnesses for horses on board:
British regiments -- three each
Hessian Regiments -- three each
Flank corps -- three each
The regiments are responsible for this

Order, Headquarters, New York
22 December 1779

The general-in-chief is greatly displeased to learn that the captains of the transport ships have been so poorly treated by the officers of the army. The general-in-chief hopes that this disgraceful conduct will be made known in published orders, in order to prevent such practice in the future.

The 23rd - Those regiments which have not yet been able to shoe their wagon horses, must have them shod by their regimental smiths, if they have such, or at the English smiths, where all necessary materials are available.

The colonel orders that when the non-commissioned officers of the guard get wood delivered, the wood is to be divided into seven equal parts, so that the guards on the sixth and seventh days will get a share, the same as those on the first day.

Mirbach Order Book

The same practice is to be observed with the wagon wood for the pickets. The non-commissioned officers are to adhere strictly to this practice.

The 24th - The soldiers on post are to receive their wood from the magazine on 24 December 1779, according to regulations.

<u>Order, Headquarters, New York
24 December 1779</u>

Captain Richardson of the Guards is appointed supernumerary aide-de-camp to General Mathew.

The 25th - Captain Simm, barracks master at this post, is to tend to all redoubts and guardhouses, and supply all of them at once with any shortages, and then submit a list of the missing items to the watch, after which it must be responsible for it, and turn it over to the relief guard. In case something is taken during a watch, or is missing, it must be reported at once by the officer or non-commissioned officer of the post, to the staff officer of the day.

As long as the colonel is ill, the captains of the day, so as not to disturb him, need not report to him or even less so, during bad weather than during good weather.

The 26th - Nothing.

The 27th - As conduct during wood cutting often creates disputes, (and that all the good wood that is felled by the companies is taken by them - that is, of

Mirbach Order Book

course, when the officer detached for the hewing of wood permits it - and the staff officers always get the worst, only the 5 carpenters are to hew the wood for the above-mentioned staff officers, by order of the Colonel, so as to put an end to further disputes, and they are always to take good wood for it, and the officer detached for the hewing of wood is to see that this order is strictly carried out.)

<u>Order, New York, 27 December 1779</u>
His Excellence Lieutenant General von Knyphausen orders that in the future, when uniform accessories are received by the barrelfull, by the regiments, battalions, and corps from the commissariat, the barrels are to be opened in the presence of the regimental quartermaster, or in his absence, by an officer, and if something is missing or spoiled, a certificate so stating is to be prepared, and sent to War Councilor Lorenz.

<u>Also the 27th</u> - On orders of His Excellence Lieutenant [General] von Knyphausen, the commanders of regiments, battalions, and corps are to pick up the money for uniforms for the officers from War Treasurer Schmidt, for each fifty Reichstalers remaining in their account. Next, the commanders are responsible that the uniform items which the officers acquire are similar, of a common grade, and paid for.

They are free to buy these items where they can

Mirbach Order Book

get them most easily and cheaply.

Also the 27th - His excellence orders that with the start of the new year, the new uniforms be worn, but when not on duty, and that the old ones be kept for work. The new ones are to be kept at much as possible for show.

Werner

The 28th - The signal for a fire alarm is a cannon shot from Fort Knyphausen. In case of an enemy attack or threat, two cannon shots are to be fired, also from Fort Knyphausen, which are to be quickly fired, one after another, at which, in both cases, the regiments and corps are to assemble at once before their cantonments.

The regiments are to submit a list to the barracks master at once as to their requirements for fire and light.

Order, New York, 28 December 1779

All deserters from the rebels are to be brought to the headquarters immediately.

The 29th - Nothing.

The 30th - General Mathew requires a report every week from the troops under his command, which is to be submitted every Monday. General von Bose orders therefore, that all the regiments and corps of his brigade submit a report every Sunday, including their artillery detachments. The adjutant is to sign these

Mirbach Order Book

reports.

All captains-at-arms and one private per company are to go into the city tomorrow to pick up the new uniform containers. They are to be brought to the barn at McGowan's Pass, and turned over to a guard post, which must be instructed that it is responsible for everything.

<u>The 30th</u> [sic] - The regiments are to submit lists of how much ball ammunition is needed, reckoned at forty rounds per man, and how much they have in excess of this amount. The loose balls are to be delivered to the ordnance store by the regiments, for which they will get a receipt. There is to be no target shooting or other firing of balls without the express permission of the general.

<u>The 31st</u> - The regiments are to submit the lists and deliver the balls to Captain Faye, against a receipt, according to the above order.

Tomorrow at nine o'clock, Captain Reichhold and Lieutenant Wiesemueller are to issue new uniforms to the companies, and the companies are to attend church parade in the new uniforms, day after tomorrow, so they must be distributed and fitted tomorrow after being received.

As the condition of the colonel's health still does not allow receiving the new year's congratulations tomorrow, none of the officers need consider visiting him. The colonel wishes each officer happiness in the

Mirbach Order Book

new year, health and well being, and extends his constant friendship.

After Orders

As all the uniforms were not brought from the city, the distribution tomorrow has been postponed, awaiting further orders.

Mirbach Order Book

1780

January

The 1st - The colonel wonders why, despite the already so often given order to take good care of the ball ammunition and loose balls, more are missing now than previously, since during the period not a single round has been fired at the enemy, and the total should be the same. Therefore he gives his strictest and final order herewith that care of the ball ammunition and loose balls will be taken, so that in the future reports of ammunition shortages, as many balls are available. Also the colonel holds the company commanders responsible, and they will have to pay for missing balls from their own money.

The 2nd - Commencing tomorrow, all reports are to be made to the colonel who orders the captain of the day, as well as the officer commanding the reserve picket, to inspect the picket at various times during the night. However, to insure that those inspections do not occur at the same time for both officers, the mentioned officers are to agree as to the time each will make his inspection. The captain of the day then is to make the morning report to the colonel.

The 3rd - His Excellency Lieutenant General von Knyphausen is pleased that the regiments which are in huts can protect their new uniforms, and they are not to wear them until deemed necessary, and until that time, leave them packed in the baggage house.

Mirbach Order Book

The 4th - At ten o'clock tomorrow morning, a hearing is to take place at McGowan's Pass for Corporal Schumann and six privates who are now in arrest.

The 5th - Nothing.

The 6th - When picking up meat tomorrow, Quartermaster Sergeant Noll is to bring the barrels of uniforms still in the baggage house with him, and leave them in the barn at McGowan's Pass with the others.

Wood is to be cut tomorrow. The companies are to send men into the woods again to cut as much wood as they can carry on their backs. Ensign Lange has overall charge and must insure that the wood cut for the company, before it is carried out of the woods, is placed in orderly stacks so that it can most easily be estimated as to how many cords there are, and that the caretaker does not get receipts for more than actually cut.

The 7th - As the four barrels with the remaining uniforms are to be brought from the city to the barn at McGowan's Pass, Captain Reichhold and Lieutenant Wiesemueller are to be there at nine o'clock, and divide these uniform items and everything pertaining thereto, into five equal parts and disperse them by lot. The company commanders are to divide them among their men. The colonel announces that when the company commanders have space, they are to store

Mirbach Order Book

the items in their quarters, if not opposed to the idea. But in such case, each uniform is to have the name [of a soldier]. If the company commanders are unable to store the items in their quarters, the uniforms are to be issued to the individuals, with the clearest understanding, to protect them as well as possible in their huts, and the colonel orders that no one is to use the uniform items until he orders it.

The 8th - The companies have until nine o'clock on Monday morning to receive the uniform accessory money for the third and fourth quarters of 1779, from the regimental quartermaster.

The new uniforms for the chasseurs and vacant units can be sent under escort with the heavy baggage by the companies at their convenience.

Those officers who have new uniforms available and do not need to buy new items with their uniform allowance, are to return the money to the regimental quartermaster next Monday, so that it can be applied to the cost of uniforms for the other officers. It is announced that the items acquired by the officers are to be of similar uniformity and must last for the full two years, so that the regiment is of similar appearance. Hats for the entire regiment excepted.

The 9th - The colonel orders that the new uniforms fit according to whether five feet, one, two, or three inches tall, and are not to be cut to size, but announces furthermore, that if the companies have other uniform

Mirbach Order Book

accessories of the missing men in the baggage house, that until Wednesday, when the meat is picked up, such items may be taken out of storage, and given to the men whom they fit. At the same time the companies, as one wagon is to go into the city before Wednesday, may pick up the uniforms for the chasseurs and missing men, and send them away at this opportunity.

At nine o'clock tomorrow a hearing is to be held at McGowan's Pass, with Captain Rodemann and Lieutenant Berner present. When the hearing is over, Lieutenant Colonel von Biesenrodt is to read the Articles of War. All those under arrest are to be brought to the guard at the Colonel's Company so that they can hear. At ten-thirty, all those so ordered according to the Articles of War, are ordered to report to Lieutenant von Biesenrodt.

The 10th - Tomorrow, wood for the staff officers and captains, as well as two cords for the four guards, of which each is to receive a half cord, is to be cut. That wood is to be cut in the Apthorp woods, and it is to be noted that it is to have a seal from the regiment, as well as from the caretaker, from Delancey's Woods.

Order, New York, 10 January

Lieutenant General von Knyphausen has ordered that each artillery detachment is to maintain a post at the cannons and the ammunition wagons.

Werner

Mirbach Order Book

<u>The 11th</u> - Two wagons are going into the city tomorrow, and the companies, as already informed, may send the uniform items and bring other things therefrom, when they have such. As stated in yesterday's orders, the artillery is to maintain a post with side arms at the cannons and ammunition wagons.

<u>The 12th</u> - General Mathew orders that the snow in the regimental redoubts be cleared out, and this is to be done after every snowfall. The posts on Harlem Creek are not to permit anyone from the countryside to cross without a pass, and those without a pass are to be arrested at once, and sent to General Mathew's quarters.

<u>The 13th</u> - The regimental quartermasters of regiments and corps which have tools for building huts are to return them at once to the engineer store.

As Mr. Apthorp has complained to the colonel that the soldiers have taken away wood cut for his own household, the colonel orders that the officer commanding the wood detail is not to permit such action, but the troops are to be held to cutting wood for themselves. If another complaint is received, the colonel will severely punish the officer.

<u>The 14th - (Copy)</u>

Most obedient subordinates, remember,

Experience has taught, that barrels sent from Hesse with uniform accessories; have had items

Mirbach Order Book

missing, other items completely damaged and unusable. As the prince's war treasury can not bear the expense, which provides no advantage from such items, there is no more economical alternative than delivering such items to all the regiments so that all can be repaired. In this manner, a pair of shoes or a shirt, in proportion to the loss, would be somewhat higher than otherwise as noted in the example below, and would always be available to the troops at the set price.

On the other hand, that in this or that regiment there would be opposition to the division, is all the less appropriate, as this would create not only inequality in consideration of the price, but that the members of the regiment would have to pay so much more for their uniform accessories than others have to pay, which is to be avoided.

Therefore I give the example that in this year, the following uniform accessories were delivered to the corps:

Unit	Shirts	Pair of Shoes
1) The Jaeger Corps	600	300
2) Linsing Grenadier Battalion	300	200
3) Landgraf Regiment	400	250
4) Ditfurth Regiment	300	400 [?]
5) Seitz Regiment	400	250
6) The others	4,000	2,000

Mirbach Order Book

Total   6,000   3,400

Which amounts for 6,000 shirts @ 24 Albus, 8 Heller to 4,625 Taler; 3,400 pair of shoes @ 1 Reichstaler, 5 Albus, 11 Heller to 4,028 Reichstaler, 20 Albus, 8 Heller.

Determined then, of the above items as reported by the auditor, that of the total, 400 shirts and 50 pairs of shoes were either missing or completely soiled. Therefore in this consideration, the regiments are to account for only 5,600 shirts and 3,350 pairs of shoes. To alleviates the losses on the other hand, each item of the first, instead of 24 Albus, 8 Heller, is to be reckoned at 26 Albus, 5 Heller, and the latter, instead of 1 Reichstaler, 5 Albus, 11 Heller, at 1 Reichstaler, 6 Albus, 5 2/3 Heller, which difference those participating can list in the uniform accessories books under the heading of damage costs, due to the condition of the shirts and shoes when received.

New York, 7 January 1780
C. Schmidt

His Excellence Lieutenant General von Knyphausen has previously approved and ordered this to be made known to the regiments, battalions, and corps.

New York, 10 January 1780
Werner

Mirbach Order Book

The 15th - As the complaints about the soldiers cutting wood, except on the days when the cutting is under an officer's supervision, are received almost daily by the colonel, he orders for the last time and strictly, that no soldier presume to cut wood except on those days when such is cut for the entire regiment. If this occurs, when apprehended, the soldier is to be subject to the most severe punishment.

The 16th - Each battalion at this post is to furnish one officer, four non-commissioned officers, one drummer, and fifty privates each evening to the reserve picket. They are to remain in their uniforms and must be prepared so that they can move out at the first alarm.

The colonel orders that the above order be strictly observed, and that officers as well as non-commissioned officers and privates, are not to leave their position, but remain always ready.

Order, Headquarters, New York
10 January 1780

The soldiers on the North River are to call back everyone who ventures onto the ice, and fire upon them if they do not return at once.

The 17th - The colonel orders the company commanders to make known today's order, given verbally, about cutting wood, to each man, and the first one who takes wood from Apthorp's or anyone else's woods, on other than authorized days, and is caught, is to be punished by running the gauntlet twelve times, without a hearing or trial.

<u>Order, Headquarters, New York</u>
<u>17 January 1780</u>

Tomorrow is the birthday of Her Majesty the Queen of England. Therefore the cannons are to be fired at Fort George at twelve o'clock. The following regiments are to report to General Mathew:

Guards, Jaeger Corps

General von Bose's Brigade - Hereditary Prince, Prince Charles, and von Mirbach Regiments, and the Loyal Americans

The following regiments are to report to General Pattison:

The 37th, 42nd, and 43rd Regiments

The 1st and 2nd Ansbach Regiments

General von Lossberg's Brigade - Leib, Landgraf, Donop, and Bose Regiments.

The 76th Regiment is to hold itself in readiness to march to Staten Island on the shortest notice. The 80th Regiment is also to be prepared to march.

<u>The 18th</u> - As Corporal Schumann left his post maliciously and without relief, he is forever demoted. This is to be made known to the regiment so that the colonel can add the admonition that every non-commissioned officer, as well as privates, can take an

Mirbach Order Book

example from the above severe punishment.

At the request of General von Bose, as long as the rivers are frozen, the general's guard is to have loaded weapons and the colonel orders that each time when the guard goes on duty, this is to be done.

<u>Order, Headquarters, New York,
17 January 1780</u>

All officers not members of the New York garrison are to return to their respective regiments.

<u>Order, Headquarters, New York
18 January 1780</u>

As complaints have been received that the corps which have been ordered to obtain their own supply of fire wood, are cutting the wood in a very un-orderly manner, and the owners of the property are not being given receipts for the amount taken away, the commanders of the corps are to order that the wood be cut properly, and the owner given a receipt, also that the wood is cut in the proper district, and at no other place.

The 44th Regiment is to make its report to General Pattison.

<u>The 19th</u> - General von Bose hopes that the von Mirbach Regiment on the North River be especially attentive during this period of ice [on the river].

Commencing tomorrow, and as long as the North

Mirbach Order Book

River remains frozen, on order of the colonel, one officer, two non-commissioned officers, one drummer, and eighteen privates are to be assigned the flag guard.

As already ordered, this evening as well as in the future, the relieving pickets, and especially that on the North River, are to be inspected by the captain of the day, or the officer from the reserve picket, as agreed upon by those officers, and each morning the captain of the day is to report to the colonel. The reserve picket, this evening as at all times, is to be prepared to move out at once, just as the entire regiment is also to be prepared for any alarm. The order concerning these activities, given on the sixteenth of this month, is again strictly repeated.

<u>The 20th</u> - General Mathew repeats again the order that the posts on the North River are not to allow anyone to cross the ice from the country without a pass, and especially at night, no one, regardless of whom it might be, is to be allowed on the ice, and the guards are to be especially vigilant.

Signals from New York

If Kingsbridge is attacked from the front. during the daytime, two cannon shots are to be fired by Fort Knyphausen; during the night, one cannon shot by Fort Knyphausen, and a rocket by Morris house.

If Kingsbridge is attacked from the North River, during the daytime, two cannon shots are to be fired by Fort Knyphausen; during the night, by two cannon shots from that place also, and by two rockets, by the Morris house.

If Kingsbridge is attacked from Harlem Creek [during the daytime], three cannon shots are to be fired by Fort Knyphausen; during the night, by three cannon shots, and also by three rockets, by the Morris house.

Continuation Signals

On orders of Lieutenant [General] Knyphausen:

If one, two, or three cannon shots are fired at McGowan's Pass, the same is to be repeated by the 37th Regiment cantonment near the Five Mile Stone, at the so-called Dove Tavern, at Murray's house on the height at Inuklenburg [?], Bunker Hill, and Fort George. And, in case the enemy attacks in force from the North or East Rivers, behind the lines at McGowan's Pass, then, if the enemy comes from the North River, four cannon shots are to be fired from the cannons at Major Bayard's house, or by the alarm cannons which are closest to the enemy's approach route, and these are to be repeated by the Greenwich Star Redoubt and Fort George.

If four or five alarm shots are fired by Fort George, the entire garrison is to fall out under arms immediately, and march to the designated alarm places.

N.B. - The signals, as recently directed in the

order from General Mathew, are cancelled and the above are to be observed.

If an attack comes from the North River, the von Mirbach Regiment is to march to Robertson's Corps at Sontien, which is cantoned by the John's house, and await further orders.

(Copy) - <u>Order, Redhouse, eight-thirty in the evening, 20 January 1780</u>

General von Bose has received the order, to order the von Mirbach Regiment to observe the strictest adherence to the signals in today's order, and that it give close attention on its left and right flanks, and also to keep the defense of McGowan's Pass in mind.

P.S. In case of an alarm tonight, the regiment is not to march to Robertson's Corps, but to remain in its cantonment and await further orders.

Regimental Order

In event of an alarm, the officer of the flag guard is to march with the flags to McGowan's Pass, and leave one non-commissioned officer and four privates behind at the colonel's quarters. No one is to leave or move out from the reserve picket, so that in case of an alarm, it can march with the captain of the day to the defense of McGowan's Pass. In accordance with the above order, the regiment is to give strict adherence to the alarm signals issued today and be prepared to

Mirbach Order Book

move out. It is to remain before its cantonment pending further orders. The runners are to have their weapons and cartridge cases with them at all times. Baurmeister's Company at the Mill is to conduct frequent patrols tonight. As the flags are to taken to McGowan's Pass by the guard, they are to remain in the two huts there and join the reserve picket.

The 21st - The von Mirbach Regiment is not to march, in case of an attack, regardless of which side it might come from, but is to remain at its cantonment and comply with yesterday evening's orders.

The weekly report is to be discontinued.

The order given to the reserve picket not to move out, and the additional order for the entire regiment to be prepared to move out, must be observed at all times in the future.

(Copy)

From the past campaign, including the exceptional deaths against the enemy, wounded, and deaths from those wounds, and the men prisoners [of war], also their uniforms and weapons lost in the campaign, also field requisitions, the regiments, battalions, and corps are to prepare the usual lists according to the 1777 format, and deliver them at the earliest possible time to the Field War Commissariat.

A simple list on the other hand, for the year 1779, of the sick, as well as those dead of wounds and deserters, for Lieutenant General von Knyphausen,

Mirbach Order Book

can be submitted to me. The dead officers and middle staff personnel are to be listed by name, also how and on what day they died, are to be noted.

Those regiments, battalion, and corps which have not yet delivered their muster rolls for 1776 to the Commissariat for adjustment, must do so at once, so that they incur no blame for negligence.

New York, 21 January 1980   - Werner

<u>The 22nd</u> - During an alarm, regardless of the cause, the reserve picket is to march at once, without further orders, to McGowan's Pass, occupy the defensive positions on the left and right, and immediately detach one non-commissioned officer and fifteen privates to the bridge on the road at that place. That non-commissioned officer is to establish a double post across the bridge on the right side of the road leading to the heights, where it can view the plain, and a single post to watch over the weapons. Upon this alarm, the officer of the flag guard is to march with the flags to McGowan's Pass at once, to the major's quarters. Lieutenant Colonel von Biesenrodt is to remain with the two companies cantoned near his quarters, Major von Wilmowsky is to remain at McGowan's Pass, and Captain Reichhold, by the companies on the hill. The Baurmeister Company is to send at once, a non-commissioned officer and ten privates, according to conditions, to reinforce

Mirbach Order Book

McGowan's Pass. All companies are to remain in front of their cantonments, and the regimental cannon are to remain in their emplacements, pending further orders. In case of necessity, the 37th Regiments is to assist this regiment. When Captain Rodemann is captain of the day, he is to send the senior officer to the Mill. The non-commissioned officers, who accompany the pickets going on duty, are to report to the captain of the day each morning at ten o'clock. He is to instruct them exactly. They are to report again during the morning if anything new has occurred, and whether or not the rivers are frozen. Then the captain is to report to the colonel.

<u>The 23rd</u> - The expression in yesterday's order-- during the alarm, regardless of the cause-- is not to be understood that the companies are to move out on receipt of an uncertain and unconfirmed report, but the expression has the meaning that such activity is not to occur until one or another alarm signal, as described in the mentioned order, is either heard or occurs.

<u>The 24th</u> - The von Mirbach Regiment must relay to McGowan's Pass all signals exactly as received from Fort Knyphausen, but without rockets.

The colonel orders that all sentries be instructed exactly concerning the alarm signals, be attentive, and immediately to report the same to the post commander when such occur.

Mirbach Order Book

Order, Headquarters, New York, 24 January 1780

The troops on York and Long Island are to have two days' provisions in their knapsacks, keep their blankets on hand, and assemble at their designated alarm places at the least alarm, in which case the regiments and corps are to leave their hautboists, one-half of their musicians, and the convalescent in their huts, under the regimental quartermasters, and a small guard to protect them.

On orders of the colonel, as stated in the above order, the regiment is to be ready. The following guards are to be retained - Marston's Wharf, the general's and hay magazine, and one non-commissioned officer and four privates at the colonel's quarters.

Tomorrow morning, the companies are to issue the new uniforms to the men, with the clear understanding that each is to protect it in his hut, as well as possible, and upon receipt of an alarm, it is to be put on. Baurmeister's Company at the Mill is to be especially alert, and send out frequent patrols. At each company the captain-at-arms and six privates, including convalescents, are to remain behind, and in case Captain Rothe does not accompany the march, he, rather than the regimental quartermaster, is to have charge of all the guards left behind.

The 25th - The ball ammunition issued to the

Mirbach Order Book

companies today is to be well cared for by the troops, and the officers are to inspect the weapons, insure that fresh flints are installed, and above all, that the weapons are serviceable. Commencing today, and while Harlem Creek is frozen, a picket of one non-commissioned and four privates is to be posted before the Harlem Mill by Captain Rodemann. Further, the colonel orders the two companies on the heights, and those at Marston's Wharf, to send out frequent patrols.

Order, Headquarters, New York
25 January 1780

No one is to be allowed to pass the army's forward posts pending further orders, without having written permission from the general, and this is not to be given except for the most necessary reason.

The 26th - All wagons, caissons, sleds, and individuals from the countryside are to be halted by General Mathew's guard, and the von Mirbach Regiment at McGowan' Pass, whether going or coming from New York, except when they have written permission from New York or Morris house.

The colonel orders that the above order be strictly adhered to and the sentries at the major's quarters, as well as those at McGowan's Pass, are to be carefully instructed about it.

Mirbach Order Book

Orders, Headquarters, 27th January 1780

His Excellence Lieutenant General von Knyphausen requests that Lieutenant Colonel Buskirk, commander of Skinner's 4th Battalion, and the officers and privates of his command be thanked, in the official orders, for their brave conduct during the attack on the enemy posts at Elizabethtown, on the night of 25 January, and no less so, Lieutenant Howard, who during this opportunity, commanded a troop of provincial dragoons, because of his excellent conduct.

The 28th - General Mathew orders that the regiments and pickets which are on the North River and Harlem Creek are to conduct patrols throughout the night, and that the posts and patrols along the North River be especially attentive for signals on the opposite shore, such as alarm signals, smoke, or rockets, and as soon as they become aware of such, to report immediately to General Mathew.

The colonel orders that the posts and patrols on the North River and Harlem Creek be especially alert, and are to pay close attention to all signals. The regiment is to be prepared to move out at all times.

The 29th - At the request of General von Bose, one non-commissioned officer and six privates are to be provided for the picket with the Jaegers at Montresor Island. Therefore, the colonel orders that they are to stay in the house where the Jaeger picket stays.

Mirbach Order Book

Captain Rodemann is to provide instructions for the non-commissioned officer, and must assemble the picket each evening at the Mill. However, so that this does not cause the regiment excessive duty, the picket of one non-commissioned officer and four privates at the Mill is to be discontinued, and two other men are to be taken from the flag guard.

The 30th - The colonel orders that the picket for Montresor Island is to depart earlier than the others, as the non-commissioned officer must always report to Captain Rodemann.

The 31st - Nothing.

Mirbach Order Book

February

The 1st - As the North River is frozen and can be crossed on foot everywhere, the colonel orders the pickets there to be alert, and for patrols to be sent out frequently.

Order, Headquarters, New York
1 February 1780

Pending further orders, the troops are to receive the following portions of side dishes, namely, two pints of peas and one pint of rice per man, instead of three pints of peas and one-half pint of oatmeal. The soldiers who approach the outposts with passes from General Pattison are to be allowed to pass despite yesterday's general order. However, at the same time, a report containing their names is to be sent to headquarters.

Order from Major General Tryon

Rebel deserters who come into the royal lines are not to be enlisted by the corps until they have been at the headquarters. Thereafter, however, both the Queen's Rangers and the Volunteers of Ireland have the right to engage the old countrymen, if they wish to take voluntary service. However, those not desiring to serve in the mentioned corps can choose the provincial unit in which they wish to serve. Deserters who were born in America have the freedom to choose

Mirbach Order Book

the provincial unit in which they wish to serve.

The 2nd, 3rd, 4th, and 5th - Nothing.

The 6th - All posts which obtain booty from detachments from those posts are to deliver it to headquarters at Morris house, where the usual payment for such is to be made. The Refugees or other corps which capture deserters from now on are to deliver them to their respective regiments, and receive one guinea for each, without the usual regimental payment.

Order, Headquarters, New York
6 February 1780

His Excellency Lieutenant General von Knyphausen wishes to make known in official orders, his thanks to Lieutenant Colonel Norton of the Guards and the officers and men of his command for their demonstrated brave conduct and dedication to duty, which led to success during the attack on the enemy posts at Young's house, near White Plains, on the third of this month, and also to the Refugees for their demonstrated bravery during this and previous opportunities.

The 7th, 8th, 9th, and 10th - Nothing.

The 11th - As the colonel has learned that often in the companies, and especially in the huts, where the soldiers' wives sell all types of liquors, non-commissioned officers and privates have been playing all sorts of card and dice games, and even tempting passing soldiers from other regiments with drinks, even taking their money. Therefore, the colonel with the strictest and most urgent orders, orders that it is forbidden for anyone to play, so the company officers and patrols are to inspect the huts frequently, in order to prevent the resulting excesses. The colonel especially advises the company commanders that the inspection be exactly carried out, and if a non-commissioned officer should be apprehended, he is to be placed in the stocks, according to the regulations, and a private is to be arrested at once, and report to the staff.

The 12th - Nothing.

The 13th - As General Mathew has been notified that some country people have passed McGowan's Pass on sleds, on the side paths to the left of the corps, on their way to New York, the von Mirbach Regiment and Robertson's Corps are to establish posts on those byways which can prevent that, and if individuals try to pass to New York, they are to be arrested immediately.

The 14th - On orders of the colonel, the companies are to complete and have ready a provisional muster list, from 25 June to 24 December, inclusive, pending the actual muster. The additional names in the mentioned lists are not to be added yet.

The 15th - Commencing tomorrow and pending

Mirbach Order Book

further orders, the officer, one non-commissioned officer, and one private are to be withdrawn from the flag guard, and only one non-commissioned officer, one drummer, and fifteen privates are to be provided for the staff guard.

All individuals, regardless of station, except officers of the army, who wish to pass the posts, and who can show passes from the general or his adjutant, are to be allowed to pass if on the roads, and not on the byways. However, those named above who can not produce a pass, and attempt to use the byways, are to be arrested at once and sent from one guard to the next, to General von Bose. However, people on the usual road, if they have no passes, are not to be arrested, but are to be turned back.

The 16th - Nothing.

The 17th - The picket of one non-commissioned officer and six privates on Montresor Island is to be discontinued after this evening.

The 18th, 19th, and 20th - Nothing.

The 21st - It is announced to the regiment that His Serene Highness has graciously promoted the previously 1st Sergeant Peternel to ensign, in the von Wissenbach Regiment.

Order to all Regiments, Battalions, and Corps

It is the gracious order of His Serene Highness that

Mirbach Order Book

no person belonging to the lower staff or commissariat is to marry in the future, without the knowledge and consent of His Excellency Lieutenant General von Knyphausen, whose approval or refusal after an investigation is to be final.

Extract of a letter from His Excellency Lieutenant General von Knyphausen to General von Bose, dated, New York, 22 February 1780

Honorable Sir, forwarded herewith is an extract of news from the gracious letter of His Serene Highness of 22 November 1779.

Ensign Unger of the von Mirbach Regiment is transferred in the same rank, to my subordinate regiment with the pay as of 1 December. Inform him of this in the event he has not yet been informed.

Extract of the gracious letter of His Serene Highness, the Landgrave, to His Excellency Lieutenant General von Knyphausen

I return to the content of my last two letters, those of 21 and 28 June, and especially to the uniform accessories, as the reported condition of the former Pauli Company is a proof of how little attention some company chiefs and commanders have given to maintaining good standards of company management within the corps in the past, and how necessary it is to strictly attend thereto, so that my constant and newly imparted and completely explicit orders are exactly observed and fully carried out. As to my clear and obvious intentions concerning the uniform accessories always being clean and in repair, the non-commissioned officers and privates must never be cheated the least bit, but on the other hand, the frequent previous complaints of the company chiefs need no longer be heard, as all known cases have shown how unfounded such complaints were, because not one of those concerning the uniform accessories on non-commissioned officer and privates has been justified, but was repaid to the company chiefs by the four Reichstalers from the treasury.

Further extract of 22 November 1779

However, it is also required of the regiments that they report to me what they wish concerning letters patent, and they must be informed, to submit their requests.

Promotions and Transfers

1) Colonel von Hachenberg is promoted to major general and commander of the Hereditary Prince Regiment.

2) Major von Prueschenck is promoted to lieutenant colonel of the Jaeger Corps.

3) Major [Matthias] von Fuchs is promoted to lieutenant colonel in the Hereditary Prince Regiment.

Mirbach Order Book

4) Captain [Peter Michael] Waldenberg is promoted to major in the same.

5) Captain Friedrich von Eschwege is promoted to major in the Landgraf Regiment.

6) Captain Hendorf is promoted to major in the Ditfurth Regiment.

7) Captain Wilmowsky is promoted to major in the Prince Charles Regiment.

8) The previously Truembach Regiment, which has been vacant until now, is given to Lieutenant General, the Marquis d'Angelelli.

9) Lieutenant General von Wissenbach and also Major General Stirn have died. The latter on 26 October, and the former on 14 November 1779.

10) Captain Werner of the Artillery Corps and Lieutenant Fuehrer of the von Knyphausen Regiment are named brigade majors, and are to assume that duty at once.

Published at New York, 20 February 1780
F. W. Werner

Copy of a letter from the War Council to Lieutenant General von Knyphausen, 27 September 1779

It has been reported here that 1st Sergeant Baetz of the Grenadier Company of the Lieutenant General's Regiment has issued drafts to many of the non-commissioned officers and soldiers of the regiment, and accepted money payments from them for drafts on his father, who is in no way solvent, and therefore those who gave their money to the mentioned Baetz stand in the way of losing it. As similar instances have often arisen previously, and as the men are at risk by such private drafts, to insure their return, the lieutenant general orders and announces, that anyone who wishes to send money to this place, should deliver it to the regimental quartermaster at the field war commissariat, and await receipt of a draft from him, because other avenues remain uncertain as to their making the proper payment.

Werner, Brigade Major

The 22nd - The regiment is notified herewith that according to correspondence received from His Serene Highness, Ensign Unger has been transferred in rank to the von Knyphausen Fusilier Regiment.

- - - - - - - -

The 23rd - Order, Headquarters, New York
The order of 24 January of this year, that the troops on York and Long Island are to keep two days' rations in their knapsacks, is cancelled. The corps convalescents who are to sail to the south with the general-in-chief, embark tomorrow under the orders of Lieutenant Schaak of the 57th Regiment.

The 24th - General von Bose repeats the long previously given order that no sutler or any other person of the Hessians is to sell rum to the English. In the event, the rum is to be confiscated, and the transgressor severely punished.

The 25th - Nothing.

The 26th - All residents who live within our lines may go to New York and return without a pass. The colonel orders that this order be observed as intended.

The 27th - Nothing.

The 28th - On orders of His Excellency Lieutenant General von Knyphausen, the previously 1st Lieutenant [Balthasar] Spangenberg of the Prince Charles Regiment, promoted to staff captain on 18 November 1779, is to perform duty as a captain, although his commission has not yet arrived.

The 29th - Nothing.

Mirbach Order Book

March, 1780

The 1st - General Mathew previously ordered that it be made known in the inns and among the sutlers of the area under his command, that he will severely punish those who sell rum, cognac, or other similar hard liquors against the express order, and without special permission in the future. However, as this has not been observed since the order was given, the general has decided even more firmly, to carry out the most severe punishment against those who sell similarly strong and debilitating drinks, either many or singly to the troops, or to the soldiers at any time, or under any pretext against or in violation of this order. The provost marshal has notified the hosts and the authorized sutlers with the warning that the rum and such is to be taken from the owner, and half given to the informant, the other half however, is to be forgiven at the general's pleasure.

The 2nd, 3rd, and 4th - Nothing.

The 5th - The sleds, which were delivered to the regiments and corps by the barracksmaster, are to be returned immediately.

As Captain Volpert has received orders to return to his regiment, General von Bose has chosen Lieutenant Becker of the Prince Charles Regiment, to serve as brigade adjutant for the time being.

Mirbach Order Book

Regimental Order

Commencing tomorrow, the recruits and clumsy individuals are to be drilled from two to four o'clock in the afternoon by an officer and two non-commissioned officers from each company, so that the men will present a clean appearance and good posture.

(Copy)   Order on Regiments, Battalions, and Corps

As one or another of the company chiefs released men from all duty, and instead of taking a replacement for the departed company wagon and tent servants from the body of troops, or at least transferring or making some of the servants batmen, or even having one or even the same individual servant work at different companies and regiments, Negroes and children are being put in their place, and being used as wagon servants. Therefore Lieutenant General von Knyphausen issues the following order to all regiments, battalions, and corps, that in the future similar and all others changes in the body of troops and the company servants, is to be completely forbidden, except with previous written requests, and subsequent permission. Also, the company servants released to the local residents are to be returned to duty, providing arrangements can be made, that without the written permission of his excellence, similar changes are not to be made in the muster rolls in the future.

Mirbach Order Book

New York, 2 March 1780
Werner, Brigade Major

<u>The 6th</u> - Nothing.

<u>The 7th</u> - The various regiments and corps are to provide work details to make road repairs at strengths which please the corps commanders. The Guards and Prince Charles Regiment are to repair the stretch from the main barrier to the quartermaster general yard, the Hereditary Prince Regiment from the quartermaster general yard to the Jaeger camp, the Jaegers from their camp to McGowan's Pass and for a set distance beyond. The Pioneers are to repair the stretch from Kingsbridge to the main barrier, and above all, the supervision along the road over which the daily reports are sent to the Morris house. One non-commissioned officer and fifteen privates are to be furnished for the above work details, and are to assemble on orders of the colonel at seven o'clock tomorrow morning, with picks and shovels at McGowan's Pass and start work.

<u>The 8th</u> - On orders of His Excellency, Lieutenant General von Knyphausen, Ensign Unger is to perform duty with this regiment, with Major Baurmeister, as he can not yet get to his regiment, and Lieutenant Werner, on the other hand, is transferred back to the Leib Company.

- - - - - - -

Mirbach Order Book

On all Regiments, Battalions, and Corps

Major Bruen has announced that due to the great decrease in royal wagon horses, it has become nearly impossible for him to obtain more for money in this region in order to replace them. Therefore, he seeks to have those in the regiments well cared for. The inconvenience which results is that the officers must obtain their own horses for transporting their baggage from the yearly forage money, and the privates must carry their own provisions and wood. This has been announced on the order of His Excellency, Lieutenant General von Knyphausen.

New York, 8 March 1780
F. W. Werner

The 9th and 10th - Nothing.

The 11th - All loaded weapons are to be unloaded, and not loaded again, pending further orders. The cartridges are to be well cared for.

The drilling of recruits and clumsy individuals is to take place each day according to the last order. The officer assigned to that duty is to command in person. The pickets on the North and East Rivers, commencing today, are to consist of one non-commissioned officer and four privates. At the same time, commencing tomorrow, the daily guard of three privates at the Mill is cancelled. Instead, three privates from the picket are to go there.

Mirbach Order Book

<u>The 12th</u> - General Mathew is very dissatisfied that the roads have not yet been repaired, and that his order was not carried out better. General von Bose therefore, highly recommends to the brigade, that as soon as weather permits, and without further reminders, the order be closely adhered to, and performed until the roads are completely fixed, especially however, they are to drain the water and leave no stones in puddles or standing water, as has previously occurred, because such places are dangerous to cross on horseback.

<u>The 13th and 14th</u> - Nothing.

<u>The 15th</u> - To the Regiments, Battalions and Corps:

(One Taler is to be put down to the men's account for small articles of equipment for the woolen breeches belonging to every second year's equipment, by order of His Excellency Lieutenant General von Knyphausen; but should the result of the enquiry made of the Commissariat at Cassel be that this is not to be done, it will be altered and the money refunded to the men.) His excellence also orders the uniform accessories accounts be prepared to the end of March of this year, fully reconciled with the men, and paid. He then awaits a written report from the regiment, battalion, and corps commanders that this has been done.

New York, 15 March 1780

<u>The 16th</u> - A packet boat is to sail to Europe in the

Mirbach Order Book

near future.

<u>The 17th</u> - Pending further orders, the army is to receive twelve ounces of pork per week instead of six ounces of butter, according to the order issued by His Excellency Lieutenant General von Knyphausen, the companies are to retain the uniform accessories accounts, so that accounts can be reconciled with the soldiers the end of March, and if the companies have not yet entered the cost of the woolen trousers at 26 Albus, 8 Heller, they may enter the one Taler authorization. If it has already been entered however, and the uniform accessories book would be too spoiled by the correction, they are to be kept at the initial rate.

Guard mount is to be held tomorrow morning at eleven-thirty, and if not expressly changed, is to occur daily at the usual place.

<u>The 18th</u> -   <u>Regimental Order</u>

The companies are to reconcile accounts with their men to the end of this month of March, pay cash to those with credits, and then complete two extracts according to the previous years' style, of which one goes to the colonel, and the other will be returned to the company, after both copies have been signed by the staff. The small [pay] books of the soldiers, in addition to the number of extracts, are to have the names of the individuals entered, as, for example:

No. 13   Drummer   N.N.

Mirbach Order Book

No. 16   Private   N.N.

<u>The 19th</u> - Nothing.

<u>The 20th</u> - The commanders of regiments and corps are especially beseeched to give strict compliance to the public proclamation of his excellence, the lieutenant general, (concerning the gardens, fences, etc.)

<u>Order, Headquarters, New York,
20 March 1780</u>

Deputy Quartermaster General Bruen has reported that the wagon horses of some regiments are completely unfit for duty; the officers of the quartermaster general department are to inspect the wagon horses of the corps in their assigned districts. Those found unserviceable are to be taken from the regiments to which assigned along with the wagons, and such corps are to haul their provisions and wood in wagons of the quartermaster general.

<u>The 21st</u> - General von Bose announces that for the pay of the non-commissioned officers and privates to the end of March, and the credits in the uniform accessories accounts, each infantry regiment can receive from the commissariat, upon presentation of an authorization receipt, 100 pounds sterling, the Jaegers 200 pounds, and the Artillery Corps fifty pounds, on Saturday evening, 25 March.

<u>The 22nd</u> - Nothing.

Mirbach Order Book

Order, Headquaraters, New York
23 March 1780

The army is to be prepared to march on the shortest notice.

Order, Headquarters, 24 March 1780

When the army marches, the troops are to receive biscuits for six days, pork for three days, and rum for one day. The corps, under orders to embark, are to issue cartridges so that each man has sixty rounds.

The 25th - Nothing.

The 26th - All information and reports, pending further orders, are to be sent to General von Bose, because General Mathew has given over his command due to health conditions.

Order from Major General Mathew - Passes signed by Brigade Major Collins of the Guards are to be treated as if signed by Major General von Bose. The same applies to orders given by him, to be carried out exactly as if given on the general's orders. The regiment is informed that the colonel has given Quartermaster Sergeant Noll the title of sergeant.

Order, Headquarters, New York
25 March 1780

His Excellence Lieutenant General von Knyphausen requests that his approbation be made known in published orders to Lieutenant Colonel

Mirbach Order Book

Howard of the Guards, Lieutenant Colonel McPherson of the 42nd Regiment, and the officers and men under their command, for the good conduct on the morning of the 23rd of this month during the fatiguing expedition to Paramus and Hackensack, and although it was not as successful as might be wished, due to unavoidable circumstances, it still provided honor to the troops. His excellence is appreciative for the dedication to duty of Lieutenants Cranton and Percy of the navy, who commanded the division of flatboats, and also of Lieutenant Hatfield of the Royal Volunteer Militia, for his bravery during this opportunity.

The 27th - All orders given by General Mathew to the various posts remain in effect. The commanding officers of the various posts are to send all deserters, reports, and flags of truce from the enemy to Major General von Bose's quarters immediately.

Orders, Headquarters, New York
27 March 1780

Each regiment under orders to embark, is to take four wagons with weapons aboard its transport ships, except for the Volunteers of the Prince of Wales, which is to take only three, and when it marches, it is to deliver bedding and cooking utensils to the barracks master of its district. Each staff officer, adjutant, and regimental quartermaster is to be allowed to take a horse aboard his transport. The officers allowed horses

Mirbach Order Book

by the regulations, but who do not have permission [to take their horses] are to leave them behind, and forage will be provided, or they can sell them to the deputy quartermaster general. The barracks master general will pay the regiments which are embarking, the credits from their furniture money.

The apportionment of transport ships for the following corps:

[Name missing - 42nd Regiment ?] - *Montague*, 340 tons; *Rising Sun*, 256 tons; *Woodlands*, 220 tons; *Admiral Gayton*, 170 tons; a total of 986 tons.

For the Ditfurth Regiment - *Christian*, 250 tons; *Concord*, 251 tons; *Hannah*, 245 tons; *Neptune*, 216 tons; a total of 962 tons.

For the Queen's Rangers - *Palliser*, 345 tons; *Two Brothers*, 330 tons; a total of 675 tons.

For the Prince of Wales American Volunteers - *New Blessing*, 256 tons; *Friendship*, 266 tons; a total of 522 tons.

For the Volunteers of Ireland - *Springfield*, 319 tons; *Huston*, 358 tons; *Selina*, 221 tons; a total of 898 tons.

For the convalescents - *Dispatch*, 201 tons.

The Irish Volunteers are to march on Wednesday, the 29th of this month, so as to be able to embark at three o'clock in the afternoon at Brooklyn Ferry.

The Ditfurth Regiment is to march on Wednesday the 29th of this month to Jamaica, and canton in the huts of the Irish Volunteers. The regiment is then to march on Thursday to Brooklyn, and embark at twelve o'clock.

The 42nd Regiment is to embark on Thursday morning at eight o'clock at the Fly Market, and the convalescents on Thursday, also.

The Prince of Wales Volunteers are to march by Thursday also, and embark at the brewery at Brooklyn Ferry at twelve o'clock.

The Queen's Rangers are to embark at twelve o'clock on Thursday at Coles Ferry, on Staten Island.

The barracks master general, on the day before the regiments march, is to designate certain persons to receive the bedding and housekeeping items from the regiments, in their quarters, and the deputy quartermaster general is to make arrangements to receive the wagons and wagon horses at the places of embarkation.

The 28th and 29th - Nothing.

(Copy) Order from General von Bose to the Deputy Barracksmaster General of this Post, the 30th
General von Bose expects the corps under his command to be supplied in a complete and orderly manner with wood from the magazine. Therefore he requests the barracks department to take such measures as are necessary to insure the usual delivery, and also that a magazine be established, so that there will be no shortage of wood in the future, and that no

further difficulties arise. However, should such occur, he will be compelled to report it to the general-in-chief.

The colonel orders that a medic is to be present at every formation.

Order, Headquarters New York
30 March 1780

The 37th Regiment is to march to New York. Major General Pattison is requested to give the necessary orders for its movement.

The von Lossberg Regiment is to march from Herricks to Flushing on the coming Saturday, and canton in the huts at that place.

The 38th Regiment is to march from Flushing to Jamaica by Saturday, and canton in the Irish Volunteer huts. Major General Smith is requested to give the necessary additional orders for its march.

The 54th, 76th, and 80th Regiments, and the von Lossberg Regiment, are to send their reports to Major General Smith at Brooklyn at once.

The 17th Dragoon Regiment, the 17th Regiment of Foot, and the 38th Regiment [are assigned] to Brigadier General Leland, who is requested to make his quarters at Jamaica.

The provincial troops on Long Island are, as previously, to submit their reports to Brigadier General DeLancey at Jamaica.

Mirbach Order Book

As soon as the regiments are embarked, each and every one is to submit a report to the deputy adjutant general in the format which was sent to them.

The officers and privates of the corps accompanying the commander-in-chief are to be ready to be embarked tomorrow morning at nine o'clock at the main guard.

The 31st - As Assistant Barracksmaster General Lieutenant Symes wishes to pay out the furniture allowance, the regiments and corps are to prepare their lists at once and submit them to him.

Order, Headquarters, New York
30 March 1780

When the Hessian regiments and corps want to get draft horses to replace those lost or unserviceable, from Quartermaster General Major Bruen, they need not, as previously sometimes happened, apply to the wagonmaster directly, or verbally to Major Bruen, but are to submit a request to the wagon master, signed by the commander wanting the horses, stating how they were lost, and who is to take the delivery, and present it to the wagonmaster.

Mirbach Order Book

April

Order, Headquarters, New York
1 April 1780

The troops which are embarked are to report any unusual circumstances to Colonel von Westerhagen on board the transport ship *Concord*.

His Excellency Lieutenant General von Knyphausen orders the regiments and corps to submit a list to him as soon as possible, as to how many men have been paid cash from the uniform accessories money through the end of the past March, and how much the men are still owed.

The 22nd Regiment is to be embarked tomorrow, the second, at ten o'clock at Denyce's Ferry, in order to cross to Staten Island, where it is to receive further orders from Brigadier General Stirling.

From the 2nd to the 7th - Nothing.

The 8th - As the muster is finally to be held on the coming Tuesday, the colonel orders that everyone make the best possible appearance.

The 9th - The colonel orders that when captured rebels are escorted in the future, the commander of the escort is to take all necessary measures to insure that they do not escape. Therefore, the cap is to be removed [from over the powder pan, allowing the weapon to be fired instantly]. The non-commissioned officer or lance corporal commanding the escort is not

Mirbach Order Book

to allow the captive out of his sight.

Headquarters, New York,
9 April 1780

Regimental baggage guards, with the stores in New York, are to consist of not more than one non-commissioned officer and six privates, in the future.

The 10th - Nothing.

The 11th -   Headquarters, New York

As various abominations have recently taken place in the vicinity of army outposts, and by persons not authorized to be there, the commanding generals in the various districts and the officers commanding the detached posts, are to send to headquarters, in arrest, all such persons discovered in such irregular behavior.

On orders of His Excellency Lieutenant General von Knyphausen, the regiments and corps are to begin drilling four times a week.

The 11th - The regiment is to fall out for muster at the usual parade ground at ten o'clock tomorrow morning. Lieutenant Wiesemueller and a competent non-commissioned officer from each company, who have no other duty, are ordered to drill the recruits and clumsy individuals. This is to begin by Tuesday, and the drill is to be conducted from eight to ten in the morning, and two to four in the afternoon.

Mirbach Order Book

<u>The 12th</u> - Headquarters, New York

His Excellency Lieutenant General von Knyphausen orders that regiments, battalions, and corps send their sick to the hospital at New York, regardless of where it may then be located, and before they become too ill, or the scurvy gets the upper hand.

The colonel orders that the regiment is to march out for drill by Friday. The Colonel's and the Lieutenant Colonel's Companies to remain below [near New York], the other three companies however, at McGowan's Pass.

<u>The 13th</u> - Major General von Bose orders that when a reserve picket moves out, another is to be designated as a reserve at once.

<u>The 13th</u> - Headquarters, New York

As General Mathew has been awarded the 62nd Regiment of Foot, Lieutenant Colonel Howard has assumed command of the Brigade of Guards, pending further orders.

<u>The 14th</u> - Nothing.

<u>The 15th</u> - A captain, two subalterns, nine non-commissioned officers, and 100 privates, all chosen men, of the von Mirbach Regiment, are to assemble in the street at Commissary Steward's quarters this evening at sundown, or about six-thirty, and await Major DuPuy's orders. The men are to take nothing with them but cooked rations for one day, and rum.

Mirbach Order Book

They are to wear their old uniforms, but not carry blankets. Therefore only healthy and robust men are to be chosen, so that they will not fall into the enemy's hands due to fatigue.

As many local residents have so much salted meat which they obtain for a very cheap price, General von Bose believes the soldiers are not eating it, but sell it for a few pence, and has ordered that no salted meat is to pass the barriers if not accompanied by a pass from Brigade Major Collins, as to the amount.

The regimental and corps commanders are also to try to get the soldiers who wish to sell it to the local residents to trade instead for vegetables, fresh meat, or flour, and to then receive a signed certificate from an officer that a portion of salted meat was traded for vegetables or such similar items. Otherwise, if found in the possession of the local residents, it will be confiscated. It is assumed that the sutlers are included, and they are also warned by the deputy provost marshal, not to sell meat nor to trade for such with the soldiers, if they can not show written permission from an officer. The regimental and corps butchers are also to be given the order, that without written permission of their commanders, they are not to buy from the soldiers, in order to make a profit from the local residents.

<u>The 16th</u> - General von Bose requests the regimental commanders to strictly forbid firing on the

streets and among the houses and huts, as a few days ago, not only was a man wounded by a shot, but soon thereafter he died from it.

<u>The 17th -</u>   <u>Headquarters, New York, 15th April 1780</u>

In order to guard against the misuse, excessive costs, and damage to government provisions, the following orders are to be observed:

The commanders of regiments, corps, and detachments are to submit weekly returns of the number of their men, wives, and children who receive provisions, to the deputy adjutant general, and another list of those on the return who are absent, and in a situation where they receive provisions in another manner, so that the commissary general is in a position to determine anyone who is receiving rations in an unauthorized manner. The officers who have charge of the following departments, namely, the adjutant general, quartermaster general, commissary general, barracks master general, engineers, artillery, department for horses for the artillery, the hospital general, and commissary general of prisoners, are to submit returns to the deputy adjutant general of the number of personnel under their direction who receive provisions, also, differentiating those who are soldiers and to which regiment they belong, and in the future, they are to pay for the provisions they draw, which was paid for previously by the army. The commissary general awaits from each department, the end of these abuses, and will show the profits therefrom to the commander-in-chief in his return every second month.

The commissary general is requested to turn his attention to insuring that in the future, his majesty's beneficence toward the wives and children does not deteriorate, but according to circumstances, is strengthened for those most deserving. This regulation is to take effect as of 25 April of this year.

Complaints have been received that the orders concerning pressing wagons and wagon horses in the countryside is not being observed. According to that order, no one is to press wagons or horses under any pretext, if not so authorized by the general commanding in the district.

The 18th - Order, Headquarters, New York

His Excellency Lieutenant General von Knyphausen desires that his satisfaction be expressed in official orders to Major DuPuy of the Hessian von Bose Regiment, for his good conduct during the attack and assault against a host of rebels, who were cantoned on the morning of the sixteenth of this month, at Hopperstown in New Jersey, and to the officers and soldiers under his command, for their good behavior at that time. His excellence is obligated to Captain von Diemar and the troop of

Mirbach Order Book

cavalry under his command, for their determined attack against some houses at that place, which were occupied by rebels. The general also thanks Lieutenant Cranton of the navy, and the officers and sailors of his command, for the good service rendered with their flatboats.

<u>The 19th -</u>   <u>Headquarters, New York</u>
As the health of the soldiers is dependent upon the attention they give to the cleanliness of their huts and quarters, the removal of filth of all types, covering the carcasses, and frequent changing of latrine locations is necessary. When the corps march away, nothing is to be left uncovered. The commanding generals and commanding officers of the various districts are requested to give the strictest orders therefore, which will result in the greatest good for the army.

<u>The 20th and 21st</u> - Nothing.

<u>The 22nd -</u>   <u>Headquarters, New York</u>
                    <u>General Robertson's Order</u>
Such wives and children as are not authorized to receive provisions in New York are to go to Newtown at once, where they can received the same, and nowhere else. Each corps is to send a non-commissioned officer with them, and he is to give the officer of the garrison regiment there a list of their

Mirbach Order Book

numbers.

- - - - - - -

Extract of correspondence from Colonel von Cochenhausen to Major General von Bose, Dated 22 April 1780

I have just received a name list from the quartermaster general department of wagon servants who drive the royal wagons, but are not soldiers nor servants hired by the regiments. The Hessian regiments and the Jaeger Corps can obtain the missing artillery as well as wagon horses, from Major Bruen, according to that list. Those no longer serviceable are to be exchanged and others received in return.

Each commander of a regiment is to submit a receipt in English, for the horses delivered.

The 23rd - Nothing.

The 24th - As complaints have been received from the deputy quartermaster general and commissary that the fields and meadows which were recently enclosed, at much expense, have had the fences pulled out and later stolen, and as those actions are in direct violation of the proclamation issued by his excellency the lieutenant general and therefore against various issued orders, General von Bose asks the regimental and corps commanders to give the strictest heed, and tell each man individually that should one be caught, he is to be severely punished.

From the 25th to the 29th - Nothing.

Mirbach Order Book

<u>The 30th</u> - Headquarters, New York

His Excellence Lieutenant General von Knyphausen orders the regiments, battalions, and corps to submit a list as to the condition of the field kettles and bottles, namely:

1) How many of each kind have already been repaired, and the total number in useable condition?

2) How many in need of repair, which has not yet happened, must be repaired first by the regiment, and

3) What is the total number actually short?

Mirbach Order Book

March, 1780

The 1st - General Mathew previously ordered that it be made known in the inns and among the sutlers of the area under his command, that he will severely punish those who sell rum, cognac, or other similar hard liquors against the express order, and without special permission in the future. However, as this has not been observed since the order was given, the general has decided even more firmly, to carry out the most severe punishment against those who sell similarly strong and debilitating drinks, either many or singly to the troops, or to the soldiers at any time, or under any pretext against or in violation of this order. The provost marshal has notified the hosts and the authorized sutlers with the warning that the rum and such is to be taken from the owner, and half given to the informant, the other half however, is to be forgiven at the general's pleasure.

The 2nd, 3rd, and 4th - Nothing.

The 5th - The sleds, which were delivered to the regiments and corps by the barracksmaster, are to be returned immediately.

As Captain Volpert has received orders to return to his regiment, General von Bose has chosen Lieutenant Becker of the Prince Charles Regiment, to serve as brigade adjutant for the time being.

Mirbach Order Book

Regimental Order

Commencing tomorrow, the recruits and clumsy individuals are to be drilled from two to four o'clock in the afternoon by an officer and two non-commissioned officers from each company, so that the men will present a clean appearance and good posture.

(Copy)   <u>Order on Regiments, Battalions, and Corps</u>

As one or another of the company chiefs released men from all duty, and instead of taking a replacement for the departed company wagon and tent servants from the body of troops, or at least transferring or making some of the servants batmen, or even having one or even the same individual servant work at different companies and regiments, Negroes and children are being put in their place, and being used as wagon servants. Therefore Lieutenant General von Knyphausen issues the following order to all regiments, battalions, and corps, that in the future similar and all others changes in the body of troops and the company servants, is to be completely forbidden, except with previous written requests, and subsequent permission. Also, the company servants released to the local residents are to be returned to duty, providing arrangements can be made, that without the written permission of his excellence, similar changes are not to be made in the muster rolls in the future.

Mirbach Order Book

New York, 2 March 1780
Werner, Brigade Major

The 6th - Nothing.

The 7th - The various regiments and corps are to provide work details to make road repairs at strengths which please the corps commanders. The Guards and Prince Charles Regiment are to repair the stretch from the main barrier to the quartermaster general yard, the Hereditary Prince Regiment from the quartermaster general yard to the Jaeger camp, the Jaegers from their camp to McGowan's Pass and for a set distance beyond. The Pioneers are to repair the stretch from Kingsbridge to the main barrier, and above all, the supervision along the road over which the daily reports are sent to the Morris house. One non-commissioned officer and fifteen privates are to be furnished for the above work details, and are to assemble on orders of the colonel at seven o'clock tomorrow morning, with picks and shovels at McGowan's Pass and start work.

The 8th - On orders of His Excellency, Lieutenant General von Knyphausen, Ensign Unger is to perform duty with this regiment, with Major Baurmeister, as he can not yet get to his regiment, and Lieutenant Werner, on the other hand, is transferred back to the Leib Company.

Mirbach Order Book

On all Regiments, Battalions, and Corps

Major Bruen has announced that due to the great decrease in royal wagon horses, it has become nearly impossible for him to obtain more for money in this region in order to replace them. Therefore, he seeks to have those in the regiments well cared for. The inconvenience which results is that the officers must obtain their own horses for transporting their baggage from the yearly forage money, and the privates must carry their own provisions and wood. This has been announced on the order of His Excellency, Lieutenant General von Knyphausen.

New York, 8 March 1780
F. W. Werner

The 9th and 10th - Nothing.

The 11th - All loaded weapons are to be unloaded, and not loaded again, pending further orders. The cartridges are to be well cared for.

The drilling of recruits and clumsy individuals is to take place each day according to the last order. The officer assigned to that duty is to command in person. The pickets on the North and East Rivers, commencing today, are to consist of one non-commissioned officer and four privates. At the same time, commencing tomorrow, the daily guard of three privates at the Mill is cancelled. Instead, three privates from the picket are to go there.

Mirbach Order Book

The 12th - General Mathew is very dissatisfied that the roads have not yet been repaired, and that his order was not carried out better. General von Bose therefore, highly recommends to the brigade, that as soon as weather permits, and without further reminders, the order be closely adhered to, and performed until the roads are completely fixed, especially however, they are to drain the water and leave no stones in puddles or standing water, as has previously occurred, because such places are dangerous to cross on horseback.

The 13th and 14th - Nothing.

The 15th - To the Regiments, Battalions and Corps:
(One Taler is to be put down to the men's account for small articles of equipment for the woolen breeches belonging to every second year's equipment, by order of His Excellency Lieutenant General von Knyphausen; but should the result of the enquiry made of the Commissariat at Cassel be that this is not to be done, it will be altered and the money refunded to the men.) His excellence also orders the uniform accessories accounts be prepared to the end of March of this year, fully reconciled with the men, and paid. He then awaits a written report from the regiment, battalion, and corps commanders that this has been done.

New York, 15 March 1780

The 16th - A packet boat is to sail to Europe in the

Mirbach Order Book

near future.

The 17th - Pending further orders, the army is to receive twelve ounces of pork per week instead of six ounces of butter, according to the order issued by His Excellency Lieutenant General von Knyphausen, the companies are to retain the uniform accessories accounts, so that accounts can be reconciled with the soldiers the end of March, and if the companies have not yet entered the cost of the woolen trousers at 26 Albus, 8 Heller, they may enter the one Taler authorization. If it has already been entered however, and the uniform accessories book would be too spoiled by the correction, they are to be kept at the initial rate.

Guard mount is to be held tomorrow morning at eleven-thirty, and if not expressly changed, is to occur daily at the usual place.

The 18th -   Regimental Order

The companies are to reconcile accounts with their men to the end of this month of March, pay cash to those with credits, and then complete two extracts according to the previous years' style, of which one goes to the colonel, and the other will be returned to the company, after both copies have been signed by the staff. The small [pay] books of the soldiers, in addition to the number of extracts, are to have the names of the individuals entered, as, for example:

    No. 13 Drummer N.N.

Mirbach Order Book

No. 16   Private   N.N.

The 19th - Nothing.

The 20th - The commanders of regiments and corps are especially beseeched to give strict compliance to the public proclamation of his excellence, the lieutenant general, (concerning the gardens, fences, etc.)

Order, Headquarters, New York, 20 March 1780

Deputy Quartermaster General Bruen has reported that the wagon horses of some regiments are completely unfit for duty; the officers of the quartermaster general department are to inspect the wagon horses of the corps in their assigned districts. Those found unserviceable are to be taken from the regiments to which assigned along with the wagons, and such corps are to haul their provisions and wood in wagons of the quartermaster general.

The 21st - General von Bose announces that for the pay of the non-commissioned officers and privates to the end of March, and the credits in the uniform accessories accounts, each infantry regiment can receive from the commissariat, upon presentation of an authorization receipt, 100 pounds sterling, the Jaegers 200 pounds, and the Artillery Corps fifty pounds, on Saturday evening, 25 March.

The 22nd - Nothing.

Mirbach Order Book

Order, Headquaraters, New York
23 March 1780

The army is to be prepared to march on the shortest notice.

Order, Headquarters, 24 March 1780

When the army marches, the troops are to receive biscuits for six days, pork for three days, and rum for one day. The corps, under orders to embark, are to issue cartridges so that each man has sixty rounds.

The 25th - Nothing.

The 26th - All information and reports, pending further orders, are to be sent to General von Bose, because General Mathew has given over his command due to health conditions.

Order from Major General Mathew - Passes signed by Brigade Major Collins of the Guards are to be treated as if signed by Major General von Bose. The same applies to orders given by him, to be carried out exactly as if given on the general's orders. The regiment is informed that the colonel has given Quartermaster Sergeant Noll the title of sergeant.

Order, Headquarters, New York
25 March 1780

His Excellency Lieutenant General von Knyphausen requests that his approbation be made known in published orders to Lieutenant Colonel

Mirbach Order Book

Howard of the Guards, Lieutenant Colonel McPherson of the 42nd Regiment, and the officers and men under their command, for the good conduct on the morning of the 23rd of this month during the fatiguing expedition to Paramus and Hackensack, and although it was not as successful as might be wished, due to unavoidable circumstances, it still provided honor to the troops. His excellence is appreciative for the dedication to duty of Lieutenants Cranton and Percy of the navy, who commanded the division of flatboats, and also of Lieutenant Hatfield of the Royal Volunteer Militia, for his bravery during this opportunity.

The 27th - All orders given by General Mathew to the various posts remain in effect. The commanding officers of the various posts are to send all deserters, reports, and flags of truce from the enemy to Major General von Bose's quarters immediately.

<u>Orders, Headquarters, New York</u>
<u>27 March 1780</u>

Each regiment under orders to embark, is to take four wagons with weapons aboard its transport ships, except for the Volunteers of the Prince of Wales, which is to take only three, and when it marches, it is to deliver bedding and cooking utensils to the barracks master of its district. Each staff officer, adjutant, and regimental quartermaster is to be allowed to take a horse aboard his transport. The officers allowed horses

Mirbach Order Book

by the regulations, but who do not have permission [to take their horses] are to leave them behind, and forage will be provided, or they can sell them to the deputy quartermaster general. The barracks master general will pay the regiments which are embarking, the credits from their furniture money.

The apportionment of transport ships for the following corps:

[Name missing - 42nd Regiment ?] - *Montague,* 340 tons; *Rising Sun,* 256 tons; *Woodlands,* 220 tons; *Admiral Gayton,* 170 tons; a total of 986 tons.

For the Ditfurth Regiment - *Christian,* 250 tons; *Concord,* 251 tons; *Hannah,* 245 tons; *Neptune,* 216 tons; a total of 962 tons.

For the Queen's Rangers - *Palliser,* 345 tons; *Two Brothers,* 330 tons; a total of 675 tons.

For the Prince of Wales American Volunteers - *New Blessing,* 256 tons; *Friendship,* 266 tons; a total of 522 tons.

For the Volunteers of Ireland - *Springfield,* 319 tons; *Huston,* 358 tons; *Selina,* 221 tons; a total of 898 tons.

For the convalescents - *Dispatch,* 201 tons.

The Irish Volunteers are to march on Wednesday, the 29th of this month, so as to be able to embark at three o'clock in the afternoon at Brooklyn Ferry.

The Ditfurth Regiment is to march on Wednesday the 29th of this month to Jamaica, and canton in the huts of the Irish Volunteers. The regiment is then to march on Thursday to Brooklyn, and embark at twelve o'clock.

The 42nd Regiment is to embark on Thursday morning at eight o'clock at the Fly Market, and the convalescents on Thursday, also.

The Prince of Wales Volunteers are to march by Thursday also, and embark at the brewery at Brooklyn Ferry at twelve o'clock.

The Queen's Rangers are to embark at twelve o'clock on Thursday at Coles Ferry, on Staten Island.

The barracks master general, on the day before the regiments march, is to designate certain persons to receive the bedding and housekeeping items from the regiments, in their quarters, and the deputy quartermaster general is to make arrangements to receive the wagons and wagon horses at the places of embarkation.

The 28th and 29th - Nothing.

(Copy) Order from General von Bose to the Deputy Barracksmaster General of this Post, the 30th
General von Bose expects the corps under his command to be supplied in a complete and orderly manner with wood from the magazine. Therefore he requests the barracks department to take such measures as are necessary to insure the usual delivery, and also that a magazine be established, so that there will be no shortage of wood in the future, and that no

Mirbach Order Book

further difficulties arise. However, should such occur, he will be compelled to report it to the general-in-chief.

The colonel orders that a medic is to be present at every formation.

Order, Headquarters New York
30 March 1780

The 37th Regiment is to march to New York. Major General Pattison is requested to give the necessary orders for its movement.

The von Lossberg Regiment is to march from Herricks to Flushing on the coming Saturday, and canton in the huts at that place.

The 38th Regiment is to march from Flushing to Jamaica by Saturday, and canton in the Irish Volunteer huts. Major General Smith is requested to give the necessary additional orders for its march.

The 54th, 76th, and 80th Regiments, and the von Lossberg Regiment, are to send their reports to Major General Smith at Brooklyn at once.

The 17th Dragoon Regiment, the 17th Regiment of Foot, and the 38th Regiment [are assigned] to Brigadier General Leland, who is requested to make his quarters at Jamaica.

The provincial troops on Long Island are, as previously, to submit their reports to Brigadier General DeLancey at Jamaica.

Mirbach Order Book

As soon as the regiments are embarked, each and every one is to submit a report to the deputy adjutant general in the format which was sent to them.

The officers and privates of the corps accompanying the commander-in-chief are to be ready to be embarked tomorrow morning at nine o'clock at the main guard.

The 31st - As Assistant Barracksmaster General Lieutenant Symes wishes to pay out the furniture allowance, the regiments and corps are to prepare their lists at once and submit them to him.

Order, Headquarters, New York
30 March 1780

When the Hessian regiments and corps want to get draft horses to replace those lost or unserviceable, from Quartermaster General Major Bruen, they need not, as previously sometimes happened, apply to the wagonmaster directly, or verbally to Major Bruen, but are to submit a request to the wagon master, signed by the commander wanting the horses, stating how they were lost, and who is to take the delivery, and present it to the wagonmaster.

Mirbach Order Book

May, 1780

The 1st, 2nd, and 3rd - Nothing.

The 4th - The colonel repeats the already frequently given order that no soldier nor his wife is to sell rum to a Hessian, and even less so to an Englander. The first to do so is to be severely punished.

The 5th - Nothing.

The 6th - Commencing tomorrow a work detail of one captain, one officer, eight non-commissioned officers, one medic, two drummers, and 120 privates, with weapons, is to be furnished at the main barrier, and two non-commissioned officers and twenty privates to Fort Knyphausen, and two non-commissioned officers and twenty privates to Morrisania.

The 7th - A picket of one captain, one officer, four non-commissioned officers, one drummer, and fifty privates is to go to Morrisania to cover the quartermaster general wagons and horses near Eagle's house.

The 8th - Nothing.

The 9th - Order, Headquarters, New York

The commanders of work details are to give strict attention to the men so that the directions of the engineers can be promptly executed, and no time lost in finishing the work.

The 10th and 11th - Nothing.

The 12th - The von Lossberg Regiment is to march

Mirbach Order Book

to Jamaica tomorrow and occupy the huts of the King's American Regiment.

The usual lists of the 200 days' pack, baggage, and forage money are to be submitted to the deputy quartermaster general at once, by the 44th and Lossberg Regiments, and the barracks master is to pay the furniture money to the mentioned regiments.

In the future, rum is no longer to be issued to the work details, if the brigade majors do not submit a detailed list from each post of the number of men, to the commissary. If the men work only a half day, they are to receive only a half ration of rum.

<u>The 13th</u> - Headquarters, New York

The troops under orders to embark are to go aboard ships on Monday.

<u>The 14th</u> - The picket at Eagle's house at Morrisania is cancelled. On the other hand, the Jaegers are to provide one officer, four non-commissioned officers, and thirty privates tonight, and pending further orders, before [Redoubt] Number 8, and establish a post there to cover the quartermaster general horses.

Headquarters, New York

The von Lossberg Regiment is to embark tomorrow at twelve o'clock at Brooklyn Ferry. The 38th Regiment is to move into camp on the heights at Brooklyn tomorrow, and leave one captain and fifty privates, pending further orders, behind at Jamaica.

The 54th Regiment is to ship over to Paulus Hook tomorrow.

Order of Major General Robertson

The non-commissioned officers and privates of the 8th, 9th, 20th, 47th, and 53rd Regiments are to embark tomorrow under the command of Captain Davis of the 53rd Regiment.

The 16th - On orders of His Excellency Lieutenant General von Knyphausen, the sections are not to advance when receiving fire from the bushes, if the regiment is in two sections. Also during an attack both sections are to fire, even though the regiment is formed in two sections.

The 17th - As His Excellency Lieutenant General von Knyphausen has ordered that the linen trousers are to be worn, General von Bose hopes that these have been made available in sufficient quantity so that they can be put on, on the coming Monday, the 22nd.

The 18th - The work detail, pending further orders, is to consist of one captain, one officer, six non-commissioned officers, two drummers, and 100 privates.

New York, Headquarters, 18th

In the future, work details are to assemble at precisely five o'clock in the morning, and work until

Mirbach Order Book

nine o'clock. They are to begin work again at three o'clock in the afternoon, and work until seven o'clock in the evening.

The 19th and 20th - Nothing.

The 21st - The linen trousers are to be worn commencing tomorrow, and the woolen ones which are part of the new uniforms, are to be taken from the men and stored in the baggage house.

The 22nd - Lieutenant Henel begins his duty as adjutant for Major General von Bose tomorrow.

The 23rd and 24th - Nothing.

The 25th - As a complaint has been received by the colonel that the soldiers of the Hessian regiments not only tear out the garden fences, but that the artillery horses have grazed on the fenced meadows and grassy area, which is against the often repeated order of the commanding general, and the often stated regimental orders that they be left alone, therefore if such a culprit is caught, he is to be punished severely.

The 26th - Nothing.

Headquarters, New York, 26 May 1780

The army horses are to be put out to pasture tomorrow, except the designated number which are to be screened at the forage office. The Ansbach and Hessian artillery horses and wagon horses, as well as those of the Hessian staff, and a number of the public departments, are to be assembled on the common near the provost, following the reveille shot tomorrow morning. Mr. Jannies, commissary of forage, will be there and allot such number for duty as he finds necessary. The rest of the army's horses, except those of the quartermaster general department which have been ordered to Staten Island, are to assemble at reveille at the quartermaster general shipyard, from which place they are to be sent to Brooklyn. Mr. Cutler, forage master, will be there to assign pastures.

N.B. - The order concerning the horses to be assembled at the quartermaster general shipyard pertains only to those from the New York district.

The 27th - His Serene Highness has been pleased to promote Major Generals von Huyn of the Leib Dragoon Regiment, and von Bischhausen of the Carabinier Regiment, to lieutenant generals of the Cavalry, but the senior major generals are to retain their seniority.

Lieutenant General von Loewenstein of the Prince Charles Regiment has been given the vacant von Minnigerode Grenadier Battalion, and at his request, Major Hendorf of the von Ditfurth Regiment has been given his discharge.

General von Bose has given the colonels the task of issuing his compliments and complete satisfaction to the regiments for the well-executed exercises, and also thanks the colonels as well as all the officers, for their demonstrated attentiveness and industry, and to

Mirbach Order Book

all the regiments for their attention and hard work.

The recent and often repeated order that no rum be sold to the English and especially not to Robinson's Corps is herewith repeated for the last time, and should anyone from Major Barclay's mentioned corps be unable to show a pass, he is to be arrested in any camp, and sent to that corps.

<u>The 28th</u> - Commencing tomorrow, a guard of two non-commissioned officers and twelve privates is to be provided to the quartermaster general department [to guard the] horses and grass in the region of Harlem.

Order, Headquarters, New York

His Excellency Lieutenant General von Knyphausen is very dissatisfied about the many complaints which he receives daily that are contrary to the issued orders to the commanders of detachments; the soldiers leave their files or sections which cause the greatest disorder and lack of discipline. Therefore his excellence finds it necessary to publicly declare to the army that for the good of the service, and to maintain better discipline, he holds the commanding officers of detachments to be responsible for all disorder of troops under their command, and to allow no soldiers to straggle from his unit. His excellence is fully convinced that when the officers look back and consider the influence of the British government, the bad situation of the well-intended subjects who have been ruined by the rebels and so badly treated by their friends, they will find it necessary to repeat the order which takes that into consideration.

Mirbach Order Book

June, 1780

The 1st - Nothing.

The 2nd - General von Bose orders the Hessian regiments to drill their clumsy individuals diligently.

Headquarters, New York, 1 June 1780

The general order of the 28th of last month is to be read by an officer to every company in the army. The heads of departments are to employ the best possible means to insure that those persons employed by them are also made aware of it.

The 3rd -   Headquarters, New York

As tomorrow is the birthday of His Majesty, a salute is to be fired from Fort George at twelve o'clock.

Major General Robertson's Order

Those men of the British regiments as well as the provincial corps, who are on leave, are to report to their regiments at once. The provincial corps, pending further orders, are to have no more than one officer, two non-commissioned officers, and two privates on recruiting duty. All those in excess of this number are to return to their regiments immediately.

The 4th - Nothing.

The 5th - As the Guards and the Hessian Jaeger Corps are to march away from here tomorrow morning

Mirbach Order Book

at seven o'clock, the duty is to be assumed for the time being by the three Hessian regiments.

The guard over the quartermaster general's grass is to be only one individual and, pending further orders, he is to be given no work detail.

The 6th - General von Bose orders that frequent patrols are to be made inside the palisades to the left and right of the main barrier. At the same time, the guards and posts before Fort Tryon are to remain alert.

Headquarters, New York

As robbery and plundering have increased so much that complaints are constantly received, commanders are therefore to take all possible measures to prevent such evils that disrupt all order and discipline. The officers under their respective commands are to be held accountable for keeping strict watch over their men. Should someone commit the least excess in stealing or plundering from a person, regardless of what it might be, and be caught, he must pay the victim the value of the stolen goods. This order is to be read to each individual so as to preclude any excuse, and to insure the closest adherence, and to prevent the least violation. This measure is extremely necessary at the present time.

The 7th -   Regimental Order
The pickets are to remain at their exact posts.

Mirbach Order Book

<u>The 8th</u> - In the event of an attack against the line on this side of Kingsbridge, two cannon shots are to be fired from Number 8, and these are to be answered by two cannon shots from Laurel Hill, and if more shots are fired, the regiment is to move out at once, and without further orders, march to Fort Knyphausen, leaving one captain, two officers, eight non-commissioned officers, two drummers, one medic, and 100 men, as well as the two regimental cannon behind, to occupy McGowan's Pass and Marston's Wharf. The guard at McGowan's Pass is to be especially alert for the cannon shots, and as soon as they are heard, report immediately to Major von Wilmowsky, who will pass the information on at once, so that the regiment can move out. The regiment then is to assemble at McGowan's Pass immediately. All the sick individuals are to be sent to the guard, and if it does not depend on only half of the remainder relieving the men of the guard, those who are capable of duty are to be issued weapons.

Captain Reichhold is to remain behind at McGowan's Pass with the 100 men, and detach one officer, two non-commissioned officers, and twenty privates to Marston's Wharf. However, if Captain Reichhold is on another command, Captain Rothe is to assume this duty.

<u>The 9th and 10th</u> - Nothing.

<u>The 11th</u> - As no weapons have been fired since the

last ball ammunition was issued, the colonel orders that the companies are to turn in as many loose balls as were short during the turn in of cartridges today, at seven o'clock tomorrow morning.

The 12th and 13th - Nothing.

The 14th - Following the receipt of incoming signals to the regiment, and as soon as the signals from Fort Knyphausen are observed by the regiment, 200 men of the regiment, without awaiting further orders from the general, are to march to Fort Knyphausen.

Signals from the *Vulture*, New York
11 June 1780

When the enemy is sighted in preparation for an attack, during the day, the English flag is to be flown from the fore top gallant masthead and a cannon fired; at night, two lanterns are to be displayed where best visible and two cannon shots fired.

When the enemy is moving, during the day, the English flag is to be flown from the main top gallant masthead and a cannon fired; at night, three lanterns are to be displayed and three cannon shots fired.

When the enemy is in force, during the day, the English flag is to be flown from the top gallant masthead and two cannon shots fired; at night, four lanterns are to be displayed and four cannon shots fired.

Mirbach Order Book

N.B. When the above signals are observed at Fort Knyphausen, the flag is to be raised there, and a cannon shot fired during the daytime; at night, the fort is to display two lanterns and fire two cannon shots.

Arrangement of ships on the North River
General Pattison, privateer, to Philippsburg
Vulture, man-of-war, to Spitting Devil
Surprise, letter-of-marque; *Townsend, Cornwallis,* and *Sea Horse*, ordinance transports, two miles south of Spitting Devil

The colonel orders therefore that the sentries, especially those at McGowan's Pass and in the outer camp, be alert for the above signals.

The 15th - The Hessian von Mirbach Regiment is to relieve its detachments and watches every 48 hours, except for the captain and officers of the ships' watch, who are to be relieved every 24 hours.

The 16th - Nothing.

The 17th - Headquarters, Charleston Neck
1 June 1780

The commanding general-in-chief congratulates the army for the progress which the corps under Earl Cornwallis has made in the interior of the land. Lieutenant Colonel Tarleton, who has been detached from the Earl with the cavalry and infantry of the Legion, caught up with the rebels after a march of

Mirbach Order Book

nearly 100 miles in two days. They rejected his proposal to surrender, and were attacked by him. One hundred seventy were cut down, and all cannons, baggage, and flags of their corps were captured. The loss suffered by the British consisted of two dead officers, and one officer, one non-commissioned officer, and twenty privates wounded.

The 18th - At the request of the commanding General Pattison, the Hessian von Mirbach Regiment is to provide one captain, two officers, eight non-commissioned officers, three drummers, and 100 privates for the guard in New York. On the other hand, all detachments in the line and the guards at For Tryon and Morris house are cancelled. The work detail continues, as ordered, today.

The 19th - As Captain Reichhold reports that he is to move with his men into the barracks, on orders of General Pattison, and no one knows when he is to be relieved or released, the colonel orders that at seven o'clock tomorrow morning, two wagons are to be sent into the city to take the guard at that place provisions and blankets from here, and two kettles per company. Therefore those items are to be brought to the huts of the Colonel's Company at six o'clock tomorrow morning. As Captain Reichhold must occupy the headquarters and West Wharf with four non-commissioned officers, and 33 privates daily, two non-commissioned officers are to be sent to help him.

Mirbach Order Book

The 20th - Nothing.

The 21st - The colonel orders that when the soldiers have leave in the city, they are to behave properly. If one is found not behaving properly, the colonel will hold the company commander solely responsible and accept no excuse.

The guard assigned to go to New York is to assemble, well-dressed and with their weapons and leather items in the best possible condition, tomorrow morning at five o'clock, at the huts of the Colonel's Company.

The 22nd and 23rd - Nothing.

The 24th - The guard for New York is to assemble at the Colonel's Company. The men are to have their hair trimmed and powdered, and especially today, have everything in the best possible condition. No one is to presume to go into the city in civilian attire, nor are the guards to be seen out of uniform on the streets of New York.

[In June 1780, the Mirbach Regiment was re-designated the Jung [Young] Lossberg Regiment.]

INDEX

ALBUS, Cornet 122 Ens 75
ANDERSON, Ernst Wilhelm Von 198
ANDRE, John 168
ANGELELLI, Marquis D 237
APTHORP, 192 Mr 185 215 90
BACHMANN, Sgt 133
BAETZ, Sgt 237 238
BAILLIVY, Leopold Amandus Von 57
BALCKE, Georg Von 2
BAR, 60
BARCLAY, Maj 280
BARDELEBEN, Gen Von 32
BARMIEST, Maj 51
BAUER, Grenadier 172 173
BAURMEISTER, 242 Maj 134 264 32 34 81
BECKER, Johann Bartholomai 49 Lt 240 262
BERNER, Hieronymus 51 Lt 166 179 214
BICKEL, Alexander Wilhelm 53
BIEDENKAPP, Capt 23
BIESENRODT, Ens Von 67 Hans Friedrich 51 Hans Moritz 50 Lt Col Von 214 225 51 Lt Von 203 Maj Von 54
BILSINGSLOEWEN ,59 Capt 84 Ens Von 68 Karl Wilhelm Von 51 Lt Von 51 Col Von 162

BISCHHAUSEN, Maj Gen Von 279
BISKAMP, Jacob 171
BLOCK, Col 53 Justus Heinrich 3
BODE, Johann Eckhard 2
BOHLEN, Karl Friedrich 147
BORCK, Col Von 47 59 Von 16
BOSE, Col Von 8 Gen Von 104 106 112 114 117 121 123 128 131 133 142 148 154 168 185 208 220 223 229 234 235 238 240 244 246 247 250 256 262 266 268 269 272 277 279 282 283 31 Karl Von 7 Maj Gen Von 101 182 248 255 260 270 278 Von 161
BOYNEBURG, Ludwig Wilhelm August Von 15
BOYNEBURGH, Ludwig Wilhelm August Von 51
BRAMER, Col 101 Lt Col 102
BRENER, Ens 68
BROESCKE, Friedrich August Von 50 Lt 51
BRUEN, Dep Qtrm Gen 246 268 Maj 140 243 260 265 Qtrm Gen Maj 252 274
BUELOW, Col Von 23
BURGOYNE, John 194

Mirbach Order Book

BUSKIRK, Lt Col 229
BUTTLAR, Col Von 1 8 Friedrich Treusch Von 101
BYRON, John 76
CALDER, Lt Col Sir Henry 126
CAMPBELL, John 126 Lt 159 Lt Col 168
CARLON, Lt 79
CARLSON, R 13
CARLSTON, Lt 184
CATHCART, Lord 152 167 68
CLARKE, Lt Col Allured 132
CLINTON, Gen 121 46 58 68 140 29 32 Sir Henry 119
COCHENHAUSEN, Col Von 127 161 167 173 184 260 Johann Friedrich Von 54
COLLINS, Brig Maj 247 256 269
CORNWALLIS, Earl 286 Lt Gen 163
CRANTON, Lt 248 259 270
CRUSE, Maj Von 23
CUTLER, Mr 279
DAVIS, Capt 277
DELANCEY, Brig 177 Brig Gen 251 273
DIEMAR, Capt 122 Capt Von 258 Col Von 35
DOERNBERG, Karl Ludwig 147
DONOP, Col Von 32 Wilhelm Henrich August Von 7

DRACH, Ens Von 68 Erhard Von 51
DRIEBE, Johann Georg 168
DUNCKER, Lt 51 59 Rudolf Wilhelm 47
DUPUY, 120 F C 129 Gen 121 Maj 121 143 255 258 3
EHRENSTEIN, Carl Von 44 Ensign Von 46 Karl Von 51
EITEL, Hans Henrich 8 Maj 54
EMMERICH, Col 89 Lt Col 115 156
ENDEMANN, Capt 57 Johann Wilhelm 50
ENGELHARD, 60
ERSKINE, Maj Gen Sir William 132 Sir William 126 William 83
ESCHTRUTH, Johann Adolf Von 2
ESCHWEGE, Ernst Von 10 Friedrich Von 237 Karl Wilhelm Von 6
EWALD, Johannes 52
FAETZ, Capt 76
FAYE, Capt 195 208
FERGUSON, Capt 122
FERRY, Werner Von 144
FEY, Ensign 51
FEYARE, Friedrich Wilhelm 50
FREUDENBERG, Maj 9
FREYENHAGEN, Wilhelm Johann Ernst 55
FRIEDRICH, Landgrave Of Hesse 6 44
FUCHS, Mattias Von 236

Mirbach Order Book

FUEHRER, Lt 237
GEORG, Ens 147
GERLAND, Hospital Administrator 26
GIESE, Johannes 168
GILSA, Ridingmaster Von 23
GOEBEL, Johann Otto 125
GOHR, Col Von 35
GOSE, Col Von 85
GOTTSCHALL, Dietrich Von 47
GRAF, Karl Wilhelm 102 Maj 125
GREEN, Lt 183
GREVE, Gottlieb 147
GROENING, Friedrich Henrich Von 53 Johannes Von 10
HACHENBERG, Capt Von 71 140 183 236
HACKENBERG, Maj Gen Von 3
HAIVESTON, Capt 123
HALZFELD, Maj 125
HANGER, Capt 202 Georg Von 66
HANSTEIN, Col Von 8
HANSTEIN, Kasper Friedrich 54
HAST, Corp 81
HATFIELD, Lt 248 270
HEDEMANN, August Ludwig Von 125
HEISTER, Leopold Von 4 Lt Gen Von 70 Von 5
HELDRING, Maj Gen 23
HELMERICH, Capt 9
HENCKE, Surgeon 201
HENDORF, Capt 237 Maj 279
HENEL, Lt 278
HERRINGEN, Heinrich Anton Von 3
HESSE, Landgrave Of 127 235
HEYMEL, Karl Philipp 7 Lt Col 9
HILLEBRAND, Maj 125
HORN, Col Von 101 32 Ens 75 Johann Ludwig Von 8
HOWARD, Lt 229 Lt Col 248 255 270
HOWE, Gen 46 57 58
HUTCHINSON, Adj Gen 112 Dep Adj Gen 141 170 177 178 180 184 Dep Adjutant Gen 191
HUYN, Col Von 23 Johann Christoph Von 10 Maj Gen Von 279
JANNIES, Mr 279
JONES, Valentine 38
JULIAT, Karl Josef 144
JUNGKENN, Col Von 8 Gen Von 62 Maj Gen Von 32 71
KEMBLE, Mr 17 18
KEMPLE, Lt Col 132
KERSTING, Georg Bernhard 47 Lt 51
KEYDEL, Col Von 101 146 Lt Col Von 54
KEYSER, Lt 36
KILIAN, Corp 203
KITZEL, Karl 9 Karl Von 6 Lt Col Von 125
KLAMBECK, Col 35

Mirbach Order Book

KLEIST, Eugen Benedikt Von 147
KLINGSOEHR, Ens 76
KLOCKHER, Riding Master 71
KNYPHAUSEN, 163 187 44 59 Gen Von 107 203 67 Lt Gen 166 222 258 Lt Gen Von 122-125 127-128 13- 133 135 137 141 152 154 157 167 171 181 182 184 196 199 207 21 211 214 217 22 224 229 232 235 237 239 241-245 247 253-255 261 263-267 269 277 280 43 45-46 52 56 7 85 Lt Von 177 Wilhelm Von 119 4
KOCH, Corp 149
KOEHLER, Johann Jacob 2 Lt Col 102
KOSPATH, Gen 148
KOSPOTH, Col Von 101 Maj Gen Von 182
KURZ, Lubert Franz 102
LANGE, Ens 212 51 Friedrich 50 Heinrich Friedrich 171 Lt Col 109
LAUCHHARD, Dr 14
LELAND, Brig Gen 178 251 273 Col 164
LENGERCKE, Georg Emanuel Von 3
LENGSFELD, Maj Von 9
LEOPOLD, Lt Col 53
LESLIE, Alexander 126
LOEWENSTEIN, Lt Gen Von 279 Wilhelm Von 15
LOOS, Col Von 93-95 99 Johann August Von 3
LOOSE, Col Von 82
LORENZ, War Councilor 104 109 127 15 19 207 21 28 34 37 44 48 60 61 62 78
LORING, Mr 195
LOSSBERG, Anton Friedrich Von 7 Col Von 8 Friedrich Wilhelm Von 4 Gen Von 176 Gen Von 183
MALLET, Louis Marie De 51
MALSBURG, Friedrich Von 144 Maj Von 55
MARSCHALL, Maj Gen Von 1
MARTIER, Arthur 126
MARTIN, Capt 161
MARTINI, Melchior 9
MATHEW, Edward 126 Gen 154 168 177 185 188 191 192 197 202 206 208 215 219 221 223 229 233 240 244 247 248 255 262 266 269 270
MAUVILLON, Professor 71
MCKAY, Mr 183
MCKENZIE, Frederick 200
MCPHERSON, Lt Col 248 270
MEDLANDS, Maj 63
MELL, Christian Philipp 58
MERCYEN, Engineer 163
MEURER, Johann Georg 171
MINNEGERODE, Friedrich Ludwig 22 Lt Col Von 54

Mirbach Order Book

MIRBACH, Gen Von 20 33 Maj Gen Von 44 Werner Von 4
MOLITOR, Lt Von 122
MONLUISANT, Louis De Foigny De 102
MOTZ, Justin Heinrich 120
MUELLER, Georg 105
MUENCHHAUSEN, Friedrich Ernst Von 10
NOLL, Johann Georg 82 Qtrm Sgt 247 Qtrm Sgt 269 Sgt 212
NORTH, Dr 190
NORTON, Lt Col 232
O'HARA, Charles 82 Gen 89
O'REILLY, Capt 79
O'RILEY, Capt 122
OSWALD, Johann Jakob 102
PATERSON, Brig Gen 178 Gen 164 Maj Gen 140
PATTISON, Gen 219 220 231 287 James 126 Maj Gen 251 Maj Gen 273
PAULI, Georg Henrich 54 Major 125
PERCY, Lt 248 270
PETERNEL, Sgt 234
PLATTE, Friedrich 58 6
PLESSEN, Karl August Von 7
POAVEL, Wanton 126
PORBECK, Capt 2 Friedrich Von 16 Lt Col 102 Lt Col Von 109
PORTER, Commissary 154 156 William 69
PREVOST, August 126
PRUESCHENCK, Maj Von 236
RALL, Johann Gottleib 5
RAWDON, Francis Lord 159 77
REICHEL, Capt 184
REICHHOLD, Capt 100 116 185 208 212 225 284 287 David 51
REINHARD, Gottfried 93
REUTING, Capt 79 Henrich Wilhelm 77
RICHARDSON, Capt 202 206
RITZMANN, Sgt 149
ROBERTSON, Gen 259 38 James 35 Maj Gen 282
ROBINSON, Col 45
RODDIGER, Johann Georg 168
RODEMANN, Capt 116 214 226 228 230 51 54 84 Johann Ludwig 50
ROMROD, C V 166 C Von 73 92 Christoph Ludwig 77 Col 59 Col Von 119 182 47 51 Karl Christian Von 47 Lt Col Von 54
ROTHE, Capt 134 227 284 63 80 Johann Melchior 51
ROTZMANN, Lt Col Von 32
ROUX, Ridingmaster 23
RUEFFER, Karl Friedrich 51
RUPPERSBERG, Wagonmaster 156
SAVAGE, Capt 176
SCHAAK, Lt 238
SCHADE, Henrich 156

Mirbach Order Book

SCHAEFFER, Johann Georg 168
SCHALLERN, Maj Von 55 58
SCHENCK, Maj 9
SCHIECK, Ernst Rudolf Von 13
SCHLOTTEN, Capt 57
SCHMIDT, C 217 Fanies 126 Gen 12 13 18 19 20 24 25 28 36 38 43 45 46 48 58 66 75-77 Lt Col Von 102 Maj 9 Maj Gen 127 176 178 Martin 4 Paymaster 67 161 War Treasurer 207 War Cashier 184
SCHOLLEN, Ludwig Von 9
SCHOTTEN, Friedrich Andreas 50
SCHRAIDT, Johann Konrad 50 Lt 51
SCHRAMM, 60
SCHREIBER, Johann Wilhelm 10 Schreiber Maj 9
SCHREIVOGEL, August Ernst Wilhelm Von 9
SCHREYVOGEL, Lt Col Von 55
SCHROEDER, Grenadier 172 173
SCHULER, Ferdinand Heinrich Von 171
SCHULTZ, Cyriacus Ludwig 171
SCHUMANN, Corp 212 219 Nicolaus 68
SEITZ, Col Von 58 Erdmann Franz Karl Von 55
SIMM, Capt 206
SMITH, Maj Gen 251 273
SPANGENBERG, Balthasar 239
SPENCER, Friedrich Theodor 124
SPROULE, Lt 123 171
STAHL, Maj Von 1 55
STAMFORD, Capt Von 54 Ludwig Friedrich Von 53
STEIN, Riding Master Von 55
STEIN ZU BARCHFELD, Johann Ludwig Ferdinand Von 58
STEWARD, Commissary 255
STIEGLITZ, Col Von 101
STIRLING, Brig Gen 253 Lt Col 109
STIRN, Johann Daniel 4 Maj Gen 127 237
STOPPEL, Scribe 78
STUECKRAD, Lt Col Von 32
SUDERLAND, Capt 68
SUTHERLAND, William 156
SYMES, Assistant Barracksmaster Gen Lt 252 274
TARLETON, Banastre 167 Lt Col 286
TODTENWARTH, Capt Von 1
TOLL, Capt Von 51 Karl Henrich Von 50
TROTT, Capt Von 55
TRUEMBACH, Maj Gen Von 101

Mirbach Order Book

TRYON, Gen 105-107 110
112 117 120 130 43 85
96 98 99 Maj Gen 231
TUMBEL, Lt Col 200
UNGER, Ens 235 238 242
264 51 Ferdinand 51
URFF, Maj Von 1
VAUGHAN, Maj Gen 132
VERNA, Capt 101 6 Capt
Von 7
VIRNAU, Rudolf Reinhard
151
VOLPERT, 161 Capt 240
262
WACKER, Johannes 151
WAGEHALS, Maj 101
WAGENHOLS, Maj 35
WAITZ, Capt Von 2
WALDENBERG, Peter
Michael 237
WANGENHEIM, Karl Ludwig
Von 147
WANGERMANN, 60
WEBERN, Capt Webern 108
Henrich Karl Von 7
WEBSTER, Lt Col 132
WEISMUELLER, Lt 149 154
WEISSENBORN, Ens 196
202 Johann Jacob 143
Sgt 196
WELCKE, Maj Gen Von 3
Werner 144 184 200 202
214 217 225 238 Brig
Maj 172 181 242 264
Capt 237 F W 237 243
265 Friedrich Wilhelm
143 Lt 242 Lt 264

WESTERHAGEN, Col Von
253 Johann August Von
10 Lt Col Von 8
Maximilian Von 7
WEZEL, Capt 102
WHIER, Commissary 186
187
WIESEMUELLER, Ens 67 Lt
208 212 254
WILLINGTON, Lt 183
WILMOWSKY, Capt 237
Emanuel Anshelm 25
Maj 12 204 Maj Von 32
134 225 35 51 80 284
WISKER, Ensign 51 Martin
Ludwig 47
WISSENBACH, Lt Gen Von
237 Maj Gen Von 101
WISSENMUELLER, Johann
Georg 51
WITTEMUS, Lt Col 71
WITTERNUX, Lt Col Von 23
WITZINGERODE, Johann
Ernst Von 147
WOELLWARTH, Col Von 8
Wolfgang Friedrich Von 6
WREDE, August Von 161
Karl August Von 52
WURMB, Capt Von 54 Carl
Von 9 Col Von 148 Karl
Von 7 Lt Col Von 189 52
54 56 Maj Von 54 55
Philipp Von 52
WUTGINAU, Capt Von 2
Heinrich Wilhelm 1

THE AUTHOR

Bruce E. Burgoyne was born 25 October 1924 in Benton Harbor, Michigan, and is married with three grown sons. His wife Marie, a Doctor of Education from the University of Southern California, is a helpful research companion and source of encouragement. Mr. Burgoyne's education includes a Master of Arts in Social Science (History, Economics, and Government) from Trinity University in San Antonio, Texas, plus course work at half a dozen other colleges and universities in America and overseas. He has also completed numerous military courses in such subjects as German language, Counterintelligence, and Public Information.

His employment, in addition to recently teaching a seminar course on the Hessians at Delaware State University, has included twenty years of military service in the Navy, Army, and Air Force, and six years as a civilian intelligence officer with the Army. During his military and civilian service he lived six years in Germany during which time he attended German language school in Oberammergau and two months of in-depth study, living in German households and undergoing Berlitz-type training. His daily duties required interviewing and interrogating in German, which further developed his knowledge of the language.

His forty years of research on the role of the Hessians in the American Revolutionary War have taken him and his wife to archives in England and Holland, as well as those in Germany and the United States, and resulted in the translation of more than 35 major Hessian documents.